Instant LEADERSHIP

PAUL BIRCH

First published in 1999

Kogan Page Limited
120 Pentonville Road
London
N1 9JN
UK

Stylus Publishing Inc.
22883 Quicksilver Drive
Sterling
VA 20166–2012
USA

British Library Cataloguing in Publication Data

A CIP record for this book is available from the British Library.

ISBN 0 7494 3026 5

Typeset by Jo Brereton, Primary Focus, Haslington, Cheshire
Printed and bound by Clays Ltd, St Ives plc

Contents

1

LEADERSHIP

I WANNA BE A LEADER

To have picked up, maybe even bought, this book you must see yourself in a leadership role; maybe now, maybe in the future. Why would you want to do this? Why would anyone want to lead?

It seems to me that there are a wide range of reasons that can be summed up by the Shakespeare quote, 'Be not afraid of greatness: some men are born great, some achieve greatness, and some have greatness thrust upon them.' In this case some are born to lead, some choose to lead and some have leadership thrust upon them.

Whether you are reading this because you are leading or will be leading, doesn't matter. Whether you are reading this because you have chosen a leadership role or had it thrust upon you, doesn't matter. What matters is that you are choosing to improve your abilities as a leader and this is a huge step.

Leadership is the sort of word that we all understand and all have the capacity to misunderstand. Look in any dictionary and you'll find many different definitions of the word 'lead', most of which have nothing whatever to do with business. Part of my aim will be to increase understanding and clear up misunderstanding. My main aim will be to make you better at leading.

A CONTRADICTION

The title of this book is a contradiction. Everybody knows that leadership is not something that is developed instantly. You are either born with leadership skills or it takes a lifetime of practice to develop them. Then again, it is often the case that what everybody knows is utter nonsense.

It is true that leadership, like any skill, is something that improves significantly with practice. It is true that leadership, like any skill, is a continuum and some will always be better than others. But, and this is a big but, it is also true that leadership, like any skill, can be taught and that the teaching need not involve years of self-denial and dedication.

Yes, 'instant' and 'leadership' can go together. By the time you have tried some of the exercises in the book you will see what I mean.

DO IT THIS WAY

There is another thing that everybody knows about leadership. There is a right way and a wrong way to do it. If you are going to learn to be a good leader then you are going to have to learn this right way.

A few years ago I was lucky enough to attend a short course in leadership arranged and run by the Parachute Regiment. I knew in advance that the Army's style of leadership would be that you'd be told to jump and the only legitimate question would be, 'How high, sir?'. This perception couldn't have been more wrong. Indeed, the essence of what they were teaching was that we all have a propensity for particular styles of leadership and that, under some circumstances, these styles could be wholly inappropriate. They were teaching the ability to spot the requirement in a particular situation and to have a range of leadership styles available to you so that you could adapt your style to suit.

There is no right way or wrong way to lead. In any situation some styles will work better than others, so the very best leaders will be those who know themselves, their people and the needs of their organization well enough to understand what will work best. They will then also need the skills to put this into effect.

So, is a book on general leadership skills a waste of time? No, there may be no right or wrong way to lead but there are certainly some pitfalls that you must avoid and some tips that will help. Many of the exercises in this book will be about avoiding pitfalls and teaching the tips.

2

LEADERSHIP AND MANAGEMENT

SO WHAT'S THE DIFFERENCE?

To many, the words 'leadership' and 'management' can be used interchangeably. For me they are very different and the differences help to define the essence of leadership. There are an alarming number of managers around who call themselves leaders and see what they are doing as leadership, when they don't have the first idea what leadership entails or what true leadership would mean to them and to their people. Conversely, there are very few true leaders who are proud to call themselves managers.

It is a broad generalization, but often managers are concerned with tasks and leaders are concerned with people. This is not to say that leaders do not focus on the task. Indeed, one thing that characterizes great leaders is that they achieve. The difference is that the leader realizes that the achievement of the task is through the goodwill and support of others, while the manager may not.

This goodwill and support is generated by seeing people as people, not as another resource to be deployed in support of the task. The role of a manager is often to organize resources to get something done. People are one of these resources and many of the worst managers treat people as just another interchangeable item. Your role as a leader is to cause others to follow a path you have laid or a vision you have created in order to achieve a task. Often the task is seen as subordinate to the vision. For instance, the overall task of an organization might be to generate profit, but a good leader will see profit as a by-product that flows from whatever aspect of their vision differentiates their company from the competition.

This is not to say that leadership is purely a business phenomenon. Most of us can think of an inspiring leader we have met in our lives who has nothing whatever to do with business. It might be a politician, it might be an officer in the armed forces, it might be a scout or guide leader, it might even have been a teacher or head teacher. Similarly, management is not a purely business phenomenon. Again, we can think of examples of people that we have met who fill the management niche in non-business organizations. In non-business organizations it should be easier to find an inspiring vision that is not money driven and will support true leadership. Unfortunately this is often not the case.

WHY LEADERSHIP?

Given that there is a difference between leadership and management, why would you want to be a leader? I have to confess to finding this section very difficult to write. It has been fundamental to my beliefs for so long that leaders achieve more than managers that justifying it means scouring deep into thoughts I haven't dredged up for years.

Managers get done what would have been done anyway. Leaders achieve things that could not have been done without them. They do this by releasing a hidden business power: the power of employees who have been empowered to achieve.

The second reason for being a leader is that there is a glass ceiling for managers. Managing can only get you so far in any organization. You will not be able to move beyond the position that allows you to rely on the skill of your boss or the support of the organization. Or, perhaps, if the Peter Principle holds true, you will be able to rise one level above this, into a position of incompetence, and no further.

The third reason is the fulfilment gained from the job you do. Being a leader is significantly more fulfilling than being a manager. Of course it can also be significantly tougher and significantly more frustrating.

The final reason has nothing to do with your wants, needs and desires. A led organization is significantly happier and livelier than a managed organization. This is reflected in the results, but that's covered in the first point above. The reason for mentioning it here is that it becomes a much, much better place for your employees to work.

AND A PLACE FOR MANAGEMENT

Before I move further into leadership I need to take a step back. I have been extolling the virtues of leaders and led organizations, but there is a necessary place for management. Management, being about organizing resources, is essential to business success. The difficulty for you as a leader is that you need to be able to straddle a wide divide and be both a leader and a manager. You need to be able to inspire with broad vision and yet still focus on small details. You need to be able to let go completely of control and yet still be in charge. You need to be able to trust yourself absolutely and yet trust your people too (even when, or especially when, they disagree with you).

Hey, look, nobody said it was going to be easy.

3

LEADERSHIP AND YOU

IT'S FUNDAMENTAL

The leadership mantle is not one that you don and remove like a fashionable coat or even a badge of office. It is a way of life. In some ways it becomes your life. As you work through the exercises in the book you will find that some are about what you do at work and the ways that you do it, but many touch on the very essence of you and the way that you live your life.

Leadership is all consuming. It takes over your thinking and most importantly your actions. Leadership is about giving a point to the working lives of others. You cannot even hope to do that unless you see a point to your own working life. And that means that you must live your life in a way that is an expression of that point. Your values as a leader, your actions as a leader, your very thoughts as a leader will permeate your organization. It is rather like Gandhi's comment, you must 'be the change you wish to create'.

FINDING THE TIME

As you read this book and look at the mass of things required of you, one of the first things that will strike you is that you don't have time for any of this. You are far too busy already and this stuff will only make things worse.

Ask yourself what you are busy with. There are exercises later that will help to sort the wheat from the chaff, but I can say with confidence now that 67.3 per cent of your current activity is a waste of time. I can say that with such confidence because I made up that statistic and it felt right enough for me to be confident about it. Actually, you probably already know some of the areas of your activity that waste time. I'm not talking about the time you spend drinking coffee or chatting. I'm talking about the real work that you do that makes no difference whatsoever to the success or failure of the enterprise.

For everything that you write, for everything that you respond to, particularly for every meeting you attend, ask yourself, 'What difference does this make to the company's results?'. If the activity is not delivering something that does this then it should be dispensed with post-haste.

Some of the things you do will be done for the benefit of internal politics. 'I have to go to that meeting; it would be career suicide not to.' Is this really true? Are there other, less time-consuming (and more honest) ways that you can demonstrate your value? If not, then you may well be a hopeless case and it may be that you'll waste your time reading this book. If so, thanks for buying it or borrowing it. Enjoy the read and we'll just hope that this can make some difference along the way.

I really hope that you aren't a hopeless case.

PIGGY IN THE MIDDLE

Some leaders are at the top of the organization. We have all at some time or another aspired to this role (I am assuming here that you are reading this book because you have leadership aspirations) in which we would be unfettered and able to do whatever we want. In reality, there are no leadership roles that are unaccountable. There is always someone to answer to.

For most of us this is obvious. We have a boss. Our boss has a boss. Our leadership role is a small cog in an enormous machine. This puts you, as a leader, in the position of piggy in the middle. Unless you have a true leader as a boss then you will need to cope with being managed in one way while leading in a totally different way. This is one of the hardest tricks of all to pull off. When you are being dumped on and micromanaged and told to do it this way, it is awfully difficult to lift your head and look away from the detail. It is awfully difficult to see the big picture. It is awfully difficult to be inspired and inspiring. Awfully difficult, but far from impossible.

From now on, every time your boss is giving you a hard time or managing the detail of what you are trying to do, lift your head and focus on your vision (if you don't have one, see exercise 6.12). Think about why you get up in the morning. What inspires you to carry on leading in the way that you do. Just because others are down in the gutter doesn't mean that you can't be looking at the stars.

4

LEADERSHIP AND OTHERS

THE L WORD

You will find as you read this book that love makes quite a few appearances. I'd like to say that I make no apologies for this, but I find myself apologizing for it all of the time. Indeed, this section is headed 'The L Word' because a good friend of mine recently took me to task for skirting around this as a business issue. She said that I would do almost anything to avoid mentioning the word love. Unfortunately, for me, love and leadership are inextricably linked and I am increasingly having to use the L word to explain successful business.

This does not mean the hearts and flowers, slushy, sentimental view of love that many of us have. It is important to note the breadth of this word. In his book, *The Four Loves*, C. S. Lewis identifies four distinct concepts of love that have moved from four different Greek words into one English one. These are: *storge*, or affection between unequals, such as a parent and child; *phileo*, or friendship between equals pursuing a common interest or goal; *eros*, the romantic and sexual love that colours much of the way we hear the word; and *agape*, the charitable or self-sacrificial love exemplified by Christ. For a leader, love will certainly mean passion. In fact, there is a line in Elizabeth Barrett-Browning's *Sonnets From The Portuguese* – 'I love thee with a passion put to use'. If you prefer to think of love as a passion put to use, then please feel free. Passion is an acceptable business word after all. Indeed, passion is a vital ingredient in successful business and successful leadership. It is not the same as love.

Another euphemism you might want to try out is the psychologist's favourite of 'unconditional positive regard'. That might suit you, too. Believe me, I have tried them all. In the end, though, for me it comes down to love, pure and anything but simple. To lead successfully you must be able to love.

THE POINT

Let me repeat something I said earlier because, for me, it is at the heart of your role as a leader. Leadership is about giving a point to the working lives of others. If and when you have done that, you have succeeded as a leader. If you have done that and supported the needs of the business then you are doubly successful. Perhaps that needs some clarification. You can give a point to the working lives of your people that is not directly in support of the business. This could take the form of making work fun or supporting charities through work or any of an infinite number of other ways. This will have an impact on performance, but will not fire or motivate your people so much as a point that is directly about them coming to work. Give them a reason to get up in the morning. Give them a reason to come to work. Give them a reason to say, 'Yes. This is why I do it!'

TRUST

Now we're getting to the heart of what leadership is about. I believe that there are two fundamental fears that hit every leader at some time or another. The first is the fear of being wrong and the second is the fear of letting go.

Being wrong is often not a big deal for most of us. We sometimes have a really important project to work on, or a decision that is make or break for our career, but they are rare. Even when they happen we often have support mechanisms around us that allow us to lay off the risk and share it with others. When you are a leader, a true leader rather than a cog in the machine, you are truly alone. You have no one to turn to but yourself. This is when trust of yourself is really tested. To what degree are you sure you are right? If you aren't absolutely sure, to what degree are you prepared to go with your intuition?

Some people find trusting themselves easy. They are often regarded as arrogant by others, usually with good cause. But then, leaders need a dose of arrogance just to allow them to function. If you are not good at trusting yourself you need to develop mechanisms that make it easier. One will be a track record of success. Another will be a support mechanism that allows you to check out ideas before launching them. The most fundamental is just doing it. Don't worry, go with the intuition and do it. After all, the worst that will happen is that you destroy the company and your career.

The other fear at the heart of leadership is the fear of letting go. This is another trust issue. In part it is related to trust of yourself. Mainly it is about trusting those you are leading. Make no mistake, for better or worse, if you want to be a leader you have to trust those you lead. No options. No get-out clauses. No caveats. You have to trust them. If you don't, you can manage them but never lead. If you do, then you may just find that they can work miracles that you never knew they had in them. In fact, I guarantee that some of them will.

Think about it. The people that work for you have active lives outside the office. Many of them lead groups of their own, scout troops, youth clubs, football teams, amateur dramatics. Many of them achieve things in their private lives that would astound you. At work they keep quiet about these because most of us are excellent at separating our private from our work lives.

When you manage to overcome the fear of letting go and you really start to trust people, you will find that they move above and beyond your highest expectations. Oh, to be sure, at first they'll mistrust you. If this is a change of behaviour then they will be looking for a catch. They'll be expecting you to pull in the reins at any moment. Eventually they will realize that you really mean this and their testing will take the form of pushing harder and harder at any limits you have imposed. The more you trust, the more they'll take. The more they take, the more they'll achieve. The more they achieve, the more you achieve. Leaders of the world let go. You have nothing to lose but your chains.

5

THE REST OF THE BOOK

If you have read any other books in the *Instant* series then you should be warned that the nature of the subject makes this one a little different. Leadership is a skill that can be improved but not entirely developed with a checklist approach. What you will find is that many of the exercises do not contain straightforward, simple exercises that you can immediately do to improve your skills. Some do, for sure, but many are intended to provoke thought and cause you to take a step back from your current ways of working in order to develop improvements. What makes this an *Instant* book is that even those exercises that take a long time to implement can be slotted in to an odd five minutes here or there – at least to make a start on an issue.

You need not read the exercises sequentially. The order is not entirely random, but neither is it entirely significant. Some activities are grouped together. So, for instance, you will find the strategy exercises following the overview of strategy. Others are dotted around to introduce variety as you read.

It is worth saying explicitly that there are a few topics that generate a wide range of exercises. One is strategy, absolutely fundamental to the leader. A second is love, an area that I feel makes leadership mean something. And a third is knowledge, knowing about the business you're in and the world around it.

If you find that there are sections together that are becoming dull because they are too similar, then move beyond them and perhaps come back. If you find that a section or group of sections is of no interest to you, then skip it. The beauty of the *Instant* format is that you can dip into those things that seem relevant. If there is something elsewhere that will be useful to support a particular section, then you should find it referenced.

Above all, remember that leadership is an attitude of mind as much as a set of skills. Many of the exercises are aimed at developing this attitude, but they will only work if you appreciate in advance that this is the intention. To lead well you must be a leader. To be a leader you must act like a leader, think like a leader and be seen by others as being a leader. Use the exercises that follow as tools to help this to happen.

6

THE EXERCISES

6.1 | *Charisma*

Preparation Find or create a role model.
Applicability Anyone who doesn't regard themselves as charismatic.
Time taken Constant attention for the next year.
Where/when Everywhere.

We've all met them haven't we? Those managers who have had the charisma by-pass operation and don't even seem to realize it. Charisma is a fundamental characteristic of the successful leader and yet it is tough to learn to be charismatic. There are, however, a number of characteristics of charismatic people that are easy to learn. Master some of these, act like a charismatic person, feel like a charismatic person, be seen as a charismatic person and, almost by accident, you will have become one.

Charismatic people make eye contact. Many who do not make easy eye contact with others find this difficult. Indeed they will look away, or close their own eyes without even realizing they are doing it. If you cannot see the reactions of the pupils of the person you are talking to, as you are talking to them, then you are not making eye contact. If you are uncomfortable doing this with strangers, practise with people you know and trust and move outwards.

Charismatic people greet strangers confidently. Many of us are shy, embarrassed or overawed when meeting people for the first time. You must not appear to be. You must be able to look them in the eye, smile and firmly shake hands (or greet in whatever way is culturally acceptable – kiss, bow, high five, etc). If you find this difficult you might try imagining them naked. It may not help, but it's almost always good for a laugh.

Charismatic people remember others – not only names but also facts about people they have met. This is a tougher one to learn, but 6.56 *Memory* might help.

Finally, learn to walk, talk and sit like a charismatic person. Find yourself a role model that you can admire as a charismatic person and watch how they walk, talk and sit. Copy them. Ideally choose a role model who doesn't work too close to you. You don't want to be seen obviously aping the boss. Before long, if you play the role of a charismatic person, others will see you this way and you may even come to believe it yourself.

Personal development	✪✪✪✪
Inspirational leadership	✪✪✪
Maintenance leadership	✪✪
Change leadership	✪✪
Creative leadership	✪✪

6.2 | *Being an inspiration*

Preparation None.
Applicability Any leader, any time.
Time taken Again, constant attention for the next year.
Where/when Anywhere.

If anything, being an inspiration is even harder than being charismatic (see 6.1). Of course a charismatic person tends to be inspirational, but this alone is not enough. What are the factors that cause others to be inspired by you? These are the qualities that would be worth a fortune if they were bottled. Short of finding the mythical shop that sells bottles of the stuff, we need to manufacture it for ourselves.

A first exercise is to learn how to be energetic. Energy is very inspirational. Apart from regular exercise (see 6.43 *Energy* and 6.44 *Get fit*) a key to energy is to raise the speed of your metabolism. A relatively simple way of doing this is to do some brisk exercise about 20 minutes after each meal. Just running up stairs or walking briskly between meetings is enough. What you must not do is sit in meetings or work at your desk during this period. That will give your digestion the opportunity to slow you down to its pace instead of you speeding it up to yours. So, for the next few days, try this exercise. If it works for you, continue with it.

Another obvious but easily overlooked key to being inspirational is being good at what you do. There is nothing that inspires so well as a role model. Doing well and doing well with integrity are fundamental. Do not overlook the last sentence. Integrity is at the heart of being inspirational. You may have admirers if you achieve, but bend your own and others' rules to breaking point and you will inspire no one.

The counter side to this coin is spotting when others are good at what they do. Being aware of others and their effect on the business will be a real source of inspiration. Think about when you last made an issue of congratulating someone. Make a point of doing so today. Then again tomorrow. Then...

The final piece of advice here is to learn to love. Love your business (see 6.5), your customers (see 6.6), your staff (see 6.7), your suppliers (see 6.8) and most importantly, yourself (see 6.9).

Personal development	✪✪✪✪
Inspirational leadership	✪✪✪✪
Maintenance leadership	✪
Change leadership	✪✪✪
Creative leadership	✪✪

6.3 | *Getting your inspiration*

Preparation Various.
Applicability Continuous throughout your role as a leader.
Time taken A lifetime.
Where/when Anywhere.

Inspiration is one of the magical words of our time. The picture of the artist or the poet waiting for inspiration to strike is a popular one. In truth, inspiration is one of those 'what goes around comes around' items in your life. If you feed the furnace it will heat the house. If you don't then you stay cold.

So, what does feeding the furnace mean? There are some obvious inputs. If you read a lot of business texts then you'll know something about modern business. If you read the newspapers regularly then you'll know what's going on in the world. For me, inspiration for a leader is far more than this. You should be feeding your soul as well as your brain. Attend the theatre or concerts regularly. Read a lot of novels as well as factual books. Visit an art gallery. Indeed, you might make a particular point of visiting galleries with exhibitions of contemporary art since this is likely to challenge as well as inspire. Then, once you have done all of this, you will need time for cogitation. That might be combined with jogging, working out in the gym or even walking the dog, but it should be time for you and you alone.

So, list now the additional reading materials and additional inputs that you would like to have if you only had the time. Now make time. You may not think so, but there are bound to be activities that you are involved in that contribute nothing to you, to your family, or to the world. If they were ditched they would create a hole that you could fill with inspirational activity. (See 6.19 *Delegation* and 6.23 *Mastering time* for more on ditching wasted time).

Personal development	✪✪✪✪
Inspirational leadership	✪✪✪✪
Maintenance leadership	✪
Change leadership	✪✪✪
Creative leadership	✪✪✪

6.4 | *Technical competence*

Preparation Little.
Applicability Continuous throughout your role as a leader.
Time taken A lifetime.
Where/when Anywhere.

There are two conflicting schools of thought on a leader's need to be technically competent. One says that you must be better at the jobs your people do than they are, and the other says that the leader has no need to be able to do the jobs of their people in order to lead.

Perversely I believe that there is a grain of truth in both of these and that both of these views are wrong. I cannot believe that in order to lead it is necessary to be able to do jobs better than your people. You have employed them for their skills and, in a larger organization, the range of skills you have employed will be vast. Having worked in computing roles in the past I have seen many systems being constrained to the lowest common denominator, which is often the manager's ability to understand the technology.

Nor can I believe that you can lead effectively unless you understand the pressures and the limitations placed upon your people. In many instances this knowledge will come about as a result of talking to them. In some instances you may decide to do their job for a while in order to experience these pressures and limitations. The watchword here is humility. If you are to try the jobs of your people it must be from the perspective that you do not and cannot know it as well as they do. Of course, humility isn't enough. They won't stand for simple humble too long – it had better get it's finger out and become competent but not expert.

As an immediate exercise, rate yourself against your staff on the technical competence needed to do their jobs. Their jobs, not yours. If you are higher than them then you should be developing them hard. If you are lower then you'd better be far higher on leadership skills. (See 6.64 *360-degree appraisals.*)

Personal development ✪✪✪
Inspirational leadership ✪✪
Maintenance leadership ✪✪✪
Change leadership ✪
Creative leadership ✪

6.5 | *Learning to love your business*

Preparation None.
Applicability Every leader.
Time taken Very little or, perhaps, a lifetime.
Where/when Everywhere.

Earlier in the book I made no apologies for using the word love. In the next few sections you are likely to grow sick of the word and your capacity to love may feel stretched to breaking. Tough – read on anyway.

If you are an entrepreneur and if your business has not taken over to the point that it is a millstone, you probably love it anyway and need to read no further. For those that aren't, then taking a lesson from entrepreneurs could be a good start. What attitudes do they have that could teach others?

For a start, the product or service matters. It is something that they have staked a lot on and they are going to make it a success. What have you staked in your current business? What are you prepared to stake? The chances are, for most people reading this, it's very little other than their time (and that often grudgingly). Can you change this? Can you stake more of yourself in this business? Can you move to a business that you can stake more of yourself in? Remember, staking yourself in the business has nothing to do with time. I have, in the past, worked with many people who spent a long time at the office but cared nothing for the company, the product or the customers. Whether this is done in order to enhance their career, out of fear or for any other reason is irrelevant. Their stake in the business is small despite their time there being long.

The second point about entrepreneurs is that the money matters. The way the business is run, what is spent and, most importantly, what is wasted, is significant to them. If those who worked for large organizations (or even some impersonal small ones) thought about the business as though it was their own there would be fewer resources wasted and business in general would be more efficient.

The exercise in this section? Think like an entrepreneur. Act like an entrepreneur. If you can't find ways to love your current business, then move on. Why should you be wasting such a significant piece of your life in something that you cannot love?

Personal development	✪✪✪✪
Inspirational leadership	✪✪✪
Maintenance leadership	✪✪
Change leadership	✪✪
Creative leadership	✪✪

6.6 | *Learning to love your customers*

Preparation None.
Applicability Every leader.
Time taken Very little or, perhaps, a lifetime.
Where/when Everywhere.

You want your customers to love you as a business so it is reasonable that you should love your customers.

Loving your customer is a little like the old adage, 'The customer is always right'. It holds true until it gets in the way. The next section is about learning to love your staff. There are often conflicts between staff and customers. How can you love them both? As an analogy (and not putting staff or customers into this category), think about loving your children. Those with more than one child know that they will sometimes fight. Sometimes you must arbitrate, sometimes you leave them to it. Ideally you encourage an atmosphere where they never feel the need to fight at all. Sorting out the squabbles does not imply loving one more than the other. It is a necessary part of the role.

So, how do you learn to love customers? It begins by ensuring that you have lots of contact. You can't imagine having a love affair or a marriage where your only contact with your partner is via third parties. For many leaders this is the relationship they have with their customers. Change that now by planning opportunities to meet with customers face to face. List them now.

The second thing you must do is actively learn from that contact. If your lover or partner had an issue with your relationship and you listened to them talk about it then ignored it, you wouldn't be surprised if it led to a deterioration in the relationship. Yet for many leaders this is how customers are seen. 'Let them moan and then take no action.' As though the objective of feedback was to let them get it off their chest. No, the objective is to show how much they mean to you by doing something about it. So, when you do meet them, take notes, make commitments and carry them through.

Personal development   ✪✪✪✪
Inspirational leadership   ✪✪✪
Maintenance leadership   ✪✪
Change leadership   ✪✪
Creative leadership   ✪✪

6.7 | *Learning to love your staff*

Preparation None.
Applicability Every leader.
Time taken Very little or, perhaps, a lifetime.
Where/when Everywhere.

And now, if you've been reading sequentially, we move predictably to learning to love your staff. Predictable that it should be here, yet very tough to do. In many ways this is tougher than loving your customers. With the customers it is enough to have a generic and general sort of love. Your staff have the disadvantage of being here, where you can see them, all of the time. It's tough to forgive the foibles of those that you see a lot of.

This is important to you so pay attention, I shall say this only once. You must learn to love those you lead if you are to be a successful leader. Once you do learn to do this – even if it is because you feel you must – you will then need to move to a position where the love is there because you want it, not because you need it in order to achieve results.

If the group of staff that you manage is small, you will be thinking by now of those in the group that no one could love, least of all you. If the group of staff that you manage is large, then you will be having the same thoughts about entire sections of the company. Well, get rid of those thoughts. You cannot play favourites in this game. You must be fair and even-handed and that applies to the ways that you love as well as to the ways that you manage.

The primary exercise in this section is much the same as the last. Spend time with your staff. Find out what their thoughts are. Find out what their needs and wants are. Find out how you are getting in the way of those needs and wants. Now find out how you can get out of the way and still achieve your vision.

Personal development	✪✪✪✪
Inspirational leadership	✪✪✪
Maintenance leadership	✪✪
Change leadership	✪✪
Creative leadership	✪✪

6.8 | *Learning to love your suppliers*

Preparation None.
Applicability Every leader.
Time taken Very little or, perhaps, a lifetime.
Where/when Everywhere.

Yes, I know, having all of these love sections together is starting to get a bit monotonous. If you need to, you could go and read a few other sections later in the book and come back to this one.

Whether you decide to act on this section or not depends upon your view of your relationship with suppliers. For some businesses this relationship is based purely on price and contract. That is, agree the specification and the price and then establish contractual relationships that ensure these. For many this is fine and they need not change.

Some businesses have established supplier relationships that are based on mutual benefit. These businesses have found that working with suppliers as partners offers a win-win that pays dividends to both parties. Some have gone as far as completely open-book accounting and even sharing the vision and goals of the organization. How far you go with this is your choice. But, if you see benefit in a partnership with suppliers, then learning to love them is an added benefit.

Again, the exercise is similar to previous sections. Get to know their wants and needs. Make sure that they are absolutely clear about yours. Find ways of meeting their wants and needs and work with them to find ways of meeting yours.

You must be clear about one thing before you start to change the relationship with your suppliers. This is not a case of paying lip service to an ideal. It is not something that you do today and then change your mind about tomorrow. Be absolutely sure that you are comfortable with all of the implications of this change because it becomes pretty much irrevocable.

Personal development   ✪✪✪✪
Inspirational leadership   ✪✪✪
Maintenance leadership   ✪✪
Change leadership   ✪✪
Creative leadership   ✪✪

6.9 | *Learning to love yourself*

Preparation Time spent thinking about you.
Applicability Any leader.
Time taken A lifetime.
Where/when Everywhere.

This is perhaps the most important and the hardest love of all. Your ability to love others springs from your ability to love yourself. Without this you will not be as strong a leader as you might be.

Very few of us ever manage to love ourselves. We often love things about ourselves or aspects of ourselves. There are some who appear to love themselves but do so in a loud, showy way. They are often hiding a deep distrust or dislike of themselves that is protected by this shell.

How do you love yourself? A good first step is to see yourself reflected in a mirror of love. What I mean by this is to find someone who loves you and talk to them about you. They will observe both positives and negatives, but will not make the love of you dependent upon either. True love is unconditional.

A second step is to get to know yourself. I have found keeping a diary is useful for me. Sometimes I write a straight account of what I have done during the day, but often I write about the deeper level of thinking and emotions that run under the activities. These writings are a real insight. A good friend of mine writes a stream-of-consciousness diary at the beginning of each day. This includes a huge number of insights into what is happening beneath the surface.

I have also found the psychological assessments and analyzes that I have been through in the course of my career to be useful. I would add a strong caveat to this. They can give you some insights but they are often treated as a modern form of voodoo or black magic. If they are useful then use them. If they disagree with what you think about yourself, be more prepared to throw away the test than your own view of yourself.

Personal development	✪✪✪✪
Inspirational leadership	✪✪✪
Maintenance leadership	✪✪
Change leadership	✪✪
Creative leadership	✪✪

6.10 | *Leadership and management*

Preparation None.
Applicability All leaders.
Time taken A few minutes, but relatively frequently.
Where/when Anywhere.

There was a chapter on leadership and management at the start of this book. Why another section on it now? The key reason is that this is an important area to get clear in your head. There are times when your management skills must excel. There are times when your leadership skills must excel. Knowing which is which will help you to be doing the right things.

I tend to think of the relationship between leadership and management on a three-dimensional grid. One dimension is task, another is people and the third is detail. There is a fairly clear line that goes diagonally across from a detailed high task and low people focus to a broad high people and low task focus. At one end of this line you are managing; at the other you are leading. Other areas of this chart are not so clear. For instance, a broad task issue may be the leadership of vision, setting the direction for the business. Then again it may just be the management task of getting a clear picture of the overview before breaking down to lower level tasks. Similarly, a detailed people issue may be the management role of making sure that pay and rations are taken care of, or it may be that as a leader you need to get down into the detail to take the right leadership actions for individuals you lead.

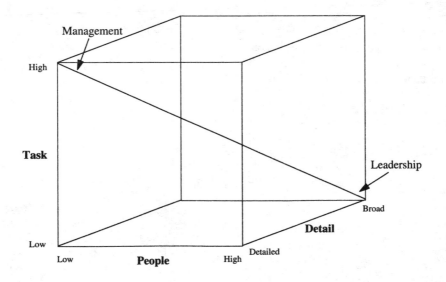

Go through the activities you have undertaken over the last week. If you have trouble remembering them, do this exercise next week after keeping a log. Evaluate what proportion of your time is management based and what proportion is leadership based.

Personal development	✪✪
Inspirational leadership	✪✪✪
Maintenance leadership	✪✪✪
Change leadership	✪✪✪
Creative leadership	✪✪

6.11 | *Strategy*

Preparation Potentially, a huge amount.
Applicability Early in your role as a leader and once every few years.
Time taken A few minutes to a few days.
Where/when Wherever you have access to any necessary data.

Giving direction through a clear strategy is one of the fundamental roles of leadership. There are entire volumes written about strategy. The strategy itself is rarely the problem. It is more often the will to implement it that lets down leaders.

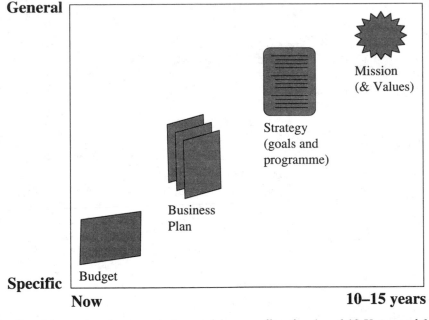

General

Mission
(& Values)

Strategy
(goals and
programme)

Business
Plan

Budget

Specific

Now

10–15 years

The first thing to develop is a mission, a vision or a direction (see 6.12 *Vision* and 6.13 *Mission*). This is the star that steers the business and sets your long-term, unattainable aspirations. From this you develop a small set of goals (6.14 *Setting goals*). These should be clear, concise, measurable, have a definite time-scale (usually five or more years) and should be discardable once the goal is achieved. Supporting each goal will be a more specific plan that will explain how the goal is made to happen. From the goals you can then develop a business plan (6.15 *Developing a business plan*). This will typically cover a three-year time-scale and will be getting quite specific. At this stage you will be attaching people to the plan and assigning individual responsibilities. From the business plan you will be able to write your next year's budget.

If you have a small business then this level of strategy will feel like overkill. The fact is, it is just as critical to your success that you know where you're going in the long term as it is to a huge bureaucracy, but the planning will take less time for a smaller business.

Read through the next few exercises and decide for yourself which will be useful and which feel like overkill. Schedule time now to go through the process of strategy development.

The final point on strategy is the one that I started with. Many businesses go through a yearly round of developing strategy where last year's plan is either ignored or altered beyond recognition. This is a sign that you are not doing the job properly. What you planned last year should feed into this year's plan. There will be changes, often huge ones. The world changes in ways that you cannot possibly anticipate. These changes should be alterations from last year's base, not a total rewrite. So, the final words – once you've written it, do it.

Personal development	✪
Inspirational leadership	✪✪✪
Maintenance leadership	✪✪✪
Change leadership	✪✪✪
Creative leadership	✪

6.12 | **Vision**

Preparation Collecting a range of magazines (possibly).
Applicability All leaders who are not already driven by a clear vision.
Time taken 10 minutes to a few days.
Where/when Anywhere.

Vision is the drive and energy that you put into your business. It is the point that you give to the working lives of those you lead. It is the thing that gets you and your people out of bed in the mornings.

Now compare that to the vision statements that most businesses concoct.

If you don't have a driving vision and you go into work primarily for the wage, then you will never inspire others, no matter how lyrical the words. If you do, then everything you do every minute of the day will convey this more surely than anything you could write.

There may be a need for writing down your vision. If your organization is large and you cannot be seen by all of your people, then your example may not convey the message to all. Writing the vision and ensuring that it is communicated will help with this.

If you feel that you are driven by a personal vision but cannot articulate it, you might try this short exercise. I have used it myself and with many others in the past and it has almost always produced results. Take a wide selection of magazines (including some you would not normally read). Go through them and rip out any images (or even phrases) that appeal to you. The appeal here is broad – forget about the vision for now. Take this pile of images and create a collage from them. Now start writing words that describe the appeal. Analyze your thinking. These words will act as a guide to what is important to you. This guide should help you to sift a vision from the things that drive you. A vision should be short. Very short. Even a single word might be enough.

Personal development   ✪✪
Inspirational leadership   ✪✪✪✪
Maintenance leadership   ✪✪✪
Change leadership   ✪✪✪
Creative leadership   ✪✪

6.13 | *Mission*

Preparation Having a vision (see 6.12).
Applicability Every leader, once every five or 10 years.
Time taken 10 minutes to a few days.
Where/when Anywhere.

There is much similarity between the vision and the mission and the terms are often used interchangeably. The mission is finite. The vision endures as long as you are leader (or until a cataclysmic shift in the nature of your business causes a rethink). The mission is achievable, but only just. The vision is phrased in a way that it is never reached. For some leaders the vision is the thing that drives them, the mission is the part of it they communicate.

Having a mission that is derived from an unreachable vision means that you can replace the mission once you reach (or get close to) the existing one. Think of NASA and their race to get a man on the moon. It drove everything they did. It defined them both internally and externally. Once they had achieved this they lost their way. It took some 30 years to get their act together again.

To create a mission, start with your vision. If you don't have and don't want a vision then you need to question why you're bothering with the mission at all. If it is just a feel-good thing or something that you think is expected of you then don't waste your time. Your people will watch what you do, not what you say or write. If you don't live the mission on a day-to-day basis it's a waste.

Make the mission a single sentence that describes a step towards achieving the unachievable. Don't worry if it seems almost impossible, this is a good thing. The time for more reality is when we move on to the goals.

Now make sure that everyone that you lead knows what your mission is and knows why it is important to you. Weigh every decision you make against this or the vision. If some of your people don't support it then they may be unnecessary. If they work against it then they are wrong.

Personal development	✪✪
Inspirational leadership	✪✪✪✪
Maintenance leadership	✪✪✪
Change leadership	✪✪✪
Creative leadership	✪✪

6.14 | *Setting goals*

Preparation Collect current metrics for the business.
Applicability All businesses.
Time taken From one day to many weeks.
Where/when Anywhere, once every year.

We are now getting into areas of measurement and shorter time-frames. This makes goals easier to understand than other aspects of strategy. They should cover a period of three to five years. This is long enough that you have time to make radical change, but short enough that you have half a chance of predicting the future.

More than about seven goals become unmanageable. Organizations that have more than this either forget the goals completely or rank them in order of importance and focus on the top few. Aside from this, if you have more than seven goals you are likely to find them conflicting with one another too often to be useful.

Each goal should be a single, measurable statement aimed three to five years in the future that seems to be half possible, half impossible. By this, I mean that you should reckon on a 50/50 chance of success (and a 50/50 chance of failure). Goals that are obviously achievable are a total waste of time. This is management, overseeing what would have been done anyway, not leadership. Goals that are obviously impossible become demotivators.

Yet again, once you have developed the goals your key task is communication. Make sure that all of the measurements that all the people throughout the organization use, are aligned with the goals.

Immediately you will hear the cry that these goals are not applicable in this or that area because it is different from the rest of the organization. There are three possible reasons for people to feel this. First, they have misunderstood their role. Help them to understand. Second, you have not got a complete set of goals. Change them. Third, it is a genuinely stand-alone part of the business that needs its own goals. Recreate it as a separate company.

Personal development   ✪
Inspirational leadership   ✪✪
Maintenance leadership   ✪✪✪✪
Change leadership   ✪✪✪
Creative leadership   ✪✪✪

6.15 | *Developing a business plan*

Preparation A developed set of goals.
Applicability All businesses.
Time taken A few hours to a few months depending upon the business.
Where/when Anywhere, every year.

Finally, we get to an area of strategy that most people are comfortable with. We understand business plans, we use them (and frequently ignore them) all of the time.

At an organization level, as opposed to a project level, a business plan lays out the next two or three years in some detail. It gives a significant amount of detail for the first year and this decreases through the life of the plan. At a project level a business plan is equivalent to the financial side of the project plan and won't be covered here.

Not only are there fairly tight measures in a business plan, there are also specific responsibilities. Without accountability the measures are useless (see 6.52 *Measurement*).

It is impossible to predict beyond the present year and yet years two and three of the plan should still be specific. Without this, the only changes your business will be able to achieve are those that can happen within a one-year time span. You might have to change your business plan after year one (indeed I will confidently predict that you will have to change it), but you will still have taken a first year's moves towards your three-year (or longer) change needs.

As an immediate exercise, study your current business plan (if it exists and if you can force it out from where it's acting as a doorstop) and write down those actions that are happening in year one that are specifically aimed at change in years two, three and beyond. If these do not constitute at least half of the actions in the plan then your focus is too short term and you need to change it.

Personal development	✪
Inspirational leadership	✪✪
Maintenance leadership	✪✪✪✪
Change leadership	✪✪✪
Creative leadership	✪✪

6.16 | *Values*

Preparation None.
Applicability Very little.
Time taken A few minutes or a lifetime of socialization.
Where/when Anywhere or nowhere.

I have very mixed feelings about values statements. One part of me thinks that some of the most meaningful statements made by businesses have been encapsulated in their values. Another part of me thinks that if you have to write it down you've lost the plot.

If every one of your actions and every decision you take is a reflection of your values – and it is – then those who work with you and for you will know quite clearly where you stand, whatever you say.

I can see two uses for values statements. First, as a statement of intent. 'These are the values that we aspire to and we recognize that we need to make the following changes in our behaviour to achieve them.' Second, as a statement of acceptable business practice from partners. 'Because these are the things we believe, these are the ways we behave and expect our business partners to behave.' The second of these sounds a little high-handed, but if you really believe in these things why would you deal with people who don't reflect your standards?

Like goals there should be few values. They need not be measurable, but they should be the sorts of things that you will recognize when you see them. They need not be specific – I have an abhorrence of values statements that are hedged about by caveats. You believe them or you don't. You can't believe them, 'as far as is appropriate in normal trading conditions' or to any other level of cop-out.

Spend some time now writing down half a dozen statements that encapsulate your beliefs about the ways you do business. If you were to publish them would they inspire? Would they be recognized in your behaviour? Would they be totally obvious? What changes could you make in your behaviour that would make your values live through your every action?

Personal development ✪
Inspirational leadership ✪✪✪
Maintenance leadership ✪✪
Change leadership ✪✪
Creative leadership ✪

6.17 | *Using stress*

Preparation None.
Applicability Any situation that induces stress.
Time taken 5 to 20 minutes.
Where/when Anywhere.

This piece is actually a series of short activities rather than one single exercise. In all leadership roles, however large or small, there is a degree of stress, but it need not be a problem.

I recently attended a seminar run by Adrian Nicholas. Adrian makes a living by jumping out of aircraft. He holds various world records for his free-diving, but also works underwater as a cave diver, has been a rally driver and has even been to the North Pole. As he says, he has been in more high-stress situations than most of us could dream of. His main piece of advice was, 'If in doubt, breathe out'. One of the first things that happens when you get stressed is that you get controlled by your breathing rather than vice versa. Breathing out (and then remembering to breathe thereafter) brings the control back to you.

Another way to control stress is to use the adrenaline by having a regular, physical workout. This could be trips to the gym. It could be taking part in a sport. It could be a brisk walk with the dog. It could even be work in the garden. Whatever it is, make sure that you break sweat and make sure that you stop thinking about your problems at work. A corollary to using the adrenaline is to learn to relax (see 6.24 *Learning to relax*).

One of the most direct ways of tackling stress is to get on and do the things that are causing it. The reason that I say this is that much stress is created by anticipating the things that cause us problems. We worsen this by putting off these activities. This causes the stress to build. Once you get on and do it then the stress goes away.

The final activity is to learn to juggle. Yes, it's daft but it works. It's hard to juggle and worry at the same time. There is no activity in this book to teach you to juggle, but there are many great books available (see Chapter 7) that make it an easy activity to master. Trust me, if I can do it, you can.

Personal development	✪✪✪✪
Inspirational leadership	✪
Maintenance leadership	✪
Change leadership	✪
Creative leadership	✪

6.18 | *Diaries*

Preparation None.
Applicability Everybody.
Time taken A few minutes a day.
Where/when Anywhere.

Every manager knows how to manage their diary. So, read no further. Then again, maybe you could pick up a tip or two.

The diary is the most useful tool most of us have and we tend to take it for granted. At least until things go wrong or it gets lost. Most of us have developed ways of working with the diary that are successful for us. Changing some of these could improve your effectiveness.

There is a close relationship between managing your diary and managing meetings (see 6.20–6.23). When you book a meeting in your diary always ask how long it will take. If the organizer can't say, ask them to give it some thought and come back with an estimate. It is unreasonable to expect you to commit your time if you don't know how much you are committing. When a meeting overruns its planned time it must be your decision whether you stay or leave. You will need to have words with the chairman or organizer of the meeting.

You should also book slots in your diary other than meetings. Time for thinking, time for creative ideas, time for your staff to drop in on you. This last one is important. I have known managers who claim to have an open-door policy, except when in meetings – and seem to spend 25 hours a day in meetings. Since your people are your primary resource for achieving your objectives, there can be very few meetings more important than giving time to them.

Go through your diary for the next few weeks. Take out the useless meetings. Add in meetings with yourself and informal drop-in times (for you to go to others and have others come to you). Also add in additional, non-meeting-based information that might be useful as reminders.

Personal development	✪✪✪✪
Inspirational leadership	✪✪
Maintenance leadership	✪✪✪
Change leadership	✪
Creative leadership	✪

6.19 | *Delegation*

Preparation Think about what you do with your days.
Applicability Anyone.
Time taken From half an hour to a day.
Where/when Anywhere, any time (but often).

Delegation is your most effective leadership tool. It is the ultimate win-win because it frees up your time and develops the people to whom you delegate. It is also an extremely tough thing to do. Strange that. Most of us would imagine that getting rid of work would be ridiculously easy.

Delegation is about trust. There is an obvious trust question – can the person that you are delegating to actually do the job? There are a number of other trust questions that are less obvious. Can this person do the job as well as I could? Will they show me up by doing it better than me? If they can do it so well, what am I here for?

Delegation is about time. It is not only about saving time by doing it, it is about creating time in order to be able to do it. It takes time to delegate and you are too busy to think about it right now. You intend to though, don't you? Maybe when your retirement party is over, you may make time to think about it. You must stop the merry-go-round now and make time to think this through.

- What do you do with your day?
- Why do you do it? (stop altogether)
- Why do you do it? (what does it add to customer?)
- Why do you do it? (give it to someone else)

There will be a large number of activities that you guard jealously and say that others can't do. ('They don't have the skills', 'It's too important', 'It's too trivial to bother', 'They are too busy already'.) All of these can be delegated. You may need to think harder about how you manage it, but they can be delegated. What you keep for yourself is about strategy and inspiration. Those must be provided by the leader.

Personal development	✪✪✪
Inspirational leadership	✪✪✪
Maintenance leadership	✪✪✪
Change leadership	✪✪✪
Creative leadership	✪✪✪

6.20 | **Meetings – and how to chair them**

Preparation Some additional work ahead of meetings.
Applicability All meetings you chair.
Time taken Less time than you currently waste.
Where/when Anywhere, any time.

For the next week, follow these meeting guidelines.

Before The Meeting

1. Try cancelling. (See 6.22 *Meetings – and how to kill them.*)
2. Objectives: what will be different at the end of the meeting as a result of it?
3. Attendees: groups of three to six work best.
4. Participants' preparation: tell them now rather than at the meeting.
5. Write an agenda. Link and order subjects. Allocate times to the agenda according to the importance of subjects, not their urgency. Keep the meeting short.
6. Other preparation. Is the venue right? Is the equipment there? Do you need to make special arrangements, such as parking or access for anyone?
7. Communicate with the participants. Do they need to attend? Ask for additional agenda items.

During The Meeting

1. START ON TIME!
2. Write up the objectives.
3. Draw attention to the times on the agenda. Reinforce the finish time.
4. Concentrate on the process (how the meeting is running) as well as the content, (what is being said).
5. Stick firmly, but not doggedly, to times on the agenda. Allow time at the start and end for social chit-chat.
6. Make sure that everyone has their say and that everyone has understood what has been said.
7. Stay focused. Take subjects out of the meeting.
8. Summarize and record specific actions and deadlines.
9. Arrange another meeting if you have to. Ideally, don't.

After The Meeting

1. Write the list of actions and deadlines.
2. Do not include those things that you wish had been said.
3. Publish within 24 hours.
4. Follow up on important action items before the deadline to check for problems.
5. If it is not remembered after the meeting then it never happened. Short meetings and clear concise action lists help memory.

Personal development	✪
Inspirational leadership	✪✪✪
Maintenance leadership	✪✪✪✪
Change leadership	✪
Creative leadership	✪

6.21 | ***Meetings – and how to develop them***

Preparation Depends upon the development you choose.
Applicability All meetings you attend.
Time taken Less time than you currently waste.
Where/when At any meeting.

Exercise 6.20 is written from the perspective of chairing meetings. You will also attend meetings. One thing you might ask yourself is how usefully your time is spent when you do. My guess is that it is not particularly useful. If it isn't, you need to do something about it.

A good start might be to take the guidelines about chairing meetings in section 6.20 and disseminate them to the chairs of other meetings you attend. They might listen, they might not. Even if they don't, they'll understand where you are coming from when you intervene.

Next, when you get an agenda for a meeting, make sure it has times for each item. If it doesn't, call up the organizer and ask for them. Next, be clear that you understand what each item is about. Ask yourself whether you need to be there at all. If you are there for only one item, ask that it be first and that you can then leave.

At the meeting, if there was no agenda, get one written up at the start. Make sure that there are times for each item and that everyone understands the purpose of it. Help the meeting to keep to time with continual reminders. If it overruns by a significant amount then leave.

This may seem like managerial detail rather than leadership overview, but it is this dross that is currently filling your days and preventing you from doing what you should be doing. One of your early tasks as a leader is to take charge of your time so that as much as possible is spent doing what you should do, not what others want you to.

Personal development	✪
Inspirational leadership	✪✪✪
Maintenance leadership	✪✪✪✪
Change leadership	✪
Creative leadership	✪

6.22 | Meetings – and how to kill them

Preparation Very little.
Applicability All meetings you attend.
Time taken Less time than you currently waste.
Where/when Any meeting.

You waste time at meetings. In some organizations, the time wasted is truly worrying. It never ceases to amaze me how unavailable many managers are. In a recent example where I was working with the board of a UK insurance firm I was told that, despite the importance of the work, the first date they could all make available was in September. This was in January! This is an extreme example, but no one can sensibly do business this way.

There are two types of meeting to kill – your's and other people's.

Your meetings are easy. Go through each that you are organizing and ask yourself what the purpose of it is. Is it intended to give information, to get information or to reach a decision? In many cases it will be a muddle of the three. In some cases it will be none of them and you'll be wondering why it hasn't been killed already. Traditional meetings are inefficient mechanisms for giving information. If necessary, arrange a short presentation session, but ideally disseminate the information another way: a way that allows others to choose when and how they absorb it. Getting information is much better done on a one-to-one basis and need not take very long at all. Decision-making usually requires people to meet (as long as they are genuinely needed for the decision). But making decisions does not take long. It is not making them that absorbs time.

Where other people's meetings are concerned, you may not worry about killing them, just avoiding them. If there are no political repercussions, just don't go. If there are, find a way around them, ideally by killing the whole meeting. If you have an altruistic streak, or if your business is being damaged by your meeting culture, then you might want to help to kill other meetings. Spend time with their organizers questioning the purpose and looking for alternatives.

Personal development	✪
Inspirational leadership	✪✪✪
Maintenance leadership	✪✪✪✪
Change leadership	✪
Creative leadership	✪

6.23 | *Mastering time*

Preparation Knowledge of what you do with your time.
Applicability All leaders.
Time taken Minutes, to save a lifetime.
Where/when Everywhere, all of the time.

There are tips elsewhere in this book for mastering your time. I would also recommend a companion volume, Brian Clegg's *Instant Time Management* (see Chapter 7).

The first thing to note about time is that it is endlessly elastic. I have a friend who is absolutely convinced that most people's lack of time is attributable to their concept of time itself. He says that you can achieve anything in any time-frame as long as you set your mind to it. He has proved this to me time and time again. Plan to achieve in impossible time-scales.

The next thing is that you do the things you want to do. Sometimes we have a perverse streak that means that there are a whole load of things that we 'should' do and which we allow to take priority, but in general we make time for what we want. Write a list of things you are not managing to do. For each item, question why it is low on your list. Certainly question why you are allowing other things to be higher. Why be busy with something if it is not delivering what you want?

Get rid of the 'should do' things. There are things you want to do and there are things you have to do in order to do the things you want. There are no 'should do' things. When you examine them, you find that the things in this category are being done to meet the expectations of others. You cannot do this and be a leader. Meet your own expectations.

Go through your 'to do' lists and diary and allocate less time to the 'have to' things and more time to the 'want to' things. Identifying which is which is an important exercise in itself.

Personal development ✪✪✪
Inspirational leadership ✪✪
Maintenance leadership ✪✪✪
Change leadership ✪
Creative leadership ✪

6.24 | *Learning to relax*

Preparation Setting some time aside.
Applicability Anyone who needs to relax more.
Time taken Only minutes, but quite often.
Where/when Anywhere, whenever you are stressed.

When you are stressed a few things happen in your body. The first is that you drug yourself. Adrenaline washes around your body getting you ready for intense physical activity that doesn't happen. Next, you release endorphins into your blood. These are morphine-like drugs that are intended to stop you feeling the pain that your body is convinced is about to happen. While this is going on, your brain processing speed is moving up and up until, very often, it gets to so many cycles per second that it is no longer functioning. This is the 'rabbit in the headlights' phase.

Set some time aside now to start. First, learn to breathe. Despite doing it all of your life the chances are you haven't got it right yet. Use your diaphragm, not your chest. You'll know that this is happening when you take a deep breath, with your hand on your stomach, and your stomach moves more than your chest. Spend a little time every so often taking deep breaths in through your nose, holding for a second and then sending them out through your mouth.

Next, sitting in a comfortable chair, starting with your toes and working slowly upwards, tense and relax muscles. Feel them relaxing and remember that feeling. Your aim is to be able to replicate that at any time. It is particularly important to concentrate on relaxing your shoulders, your hands and your stomach.

Then spend time burning off the adrenaline through physical activity.

Finally, consider seeking some outside help. I don't mean the services of a shrink (but live like you want to live). I mean a masseur/masseuse, or maybe a Tai Chi class, maybe the church, or perhaps an alternative medicine practitioner such as a homeopath or a Reiki healer.

Personal development	✪✪✪✪
Inspirational leadership	✪
Maintenance leadership	✪
Change leadership	✪
Creative leadership	✪

6.25 | *Sleep well*

Preparation None.
Applicability Anyone who has ever looked at the clock too often in the night.
Time taken Very little.
Where/when At night (mostly).

I rarely lose a night's sleep. This puts me at the top of some people's hate list. Isn't it galling when you've tossed and turned all night and some bright spark says, 'Oh, I always fall asleep as soon as my head touches the pillow'. Well, now is your chance to join this hated group.

The first most important and most useless piece of advice is don't worry about it. Important because this is the main cause of being awake – worrying about being awake. Useless because it's not easy to switch off the worry.

The tips in 6.24 *Learning to relax* will be useful, particularly the tense and relax exercise once you are in bed. Tonight and for the next few nights, follow these simple tips.

Develop a routine that is associated with going to bed. This is also particularly useful for those who normally sleep well but are occasionally thrown off centre.

Don't do physical exercise immediately ahead of going to bed. A work-out will help you to sleep, but you need time to relax afterwards for it to be effective. If you take part in very gentle exercise, such as Tai Chi, this could be done as part of a bed-time routine without keeping you awake and the relaxation it offers will be a real benefit.

Finally, once you are in bed, you have gone through your routine, you have tensed and relaxed and you are staring at the ceiling, invent a routine that will bore your brain into submission. I have never found that counting sheep works for me. I guess having a farm with a couple of hundred of them makes it something I need to stay awake for. *In extremis*, I have two routines that work for me. One is imagining a piece of jet-black velvet. It is tough to do because, as soon as your mind starts getting bored, it throws in distractions. Ignore them and focus. Another is imagining falling down a totally black, bottomless pit. Again, ignore the distractions on the way and keep on falling.

Personal development	✪✪✪✪
Inspirational leadership	✪
Maintenance leadership	✪
Change leadership	✪
Creative leadership	✪

6.26 | *Taking responsibility*

Preparation None.
Applicability Non-stop.
Time taken All of the time you have and more.
Where/when Everywhere.

Many years ago I was given a piece of advice that keeps coming back to haunt me. I was told that every time I point my finger at someone else, there are three fingers pointing back at me. Yes, it's trite and cutesy, but it is sticks in my mind to a degree that really frustrates me.

As a leader, when one of your people screws up, it is your fault. When one of your people does well, they get the praise. Before you start bemoaning the injustice of this, remember that you have a choice. You are playing this role because you have chosen to. You could back out of that choice at any time.

One of your main roles as a leader is to take the flak that would hit your people and to redirect the praise that might miss them. This calls for a combination of tough skin and open heart that is very difficult to maintain. Yet again, nobody said it was going to be easy.

As if this wasn't tough enough, taking responsibility doesn't stop there. You are responsible for everything your organization does whether it falls into your area of official responsibility or not. If, for instance, a customer calls and their problem sits elsewhere in the organization, the last thing you should do is tell them that. Take responsibility for the problem and sort it out for them. This is easy to see when the customer calls directly, but when a problem occurs elsewhere that is less directly linked to an individual customer your knee-jerk reaction should be to ask how you can fix it. If something isn't working in your business it is your problem. No arguments, no prevarication – fix it.

Collect together a sample set of customer complaint letters. Identify the proportion of customers that would have been mollified, or even delighted, by being sorted out by the first person they contacted. Find a way to spread this learning.

Personal development	✪✪
Inspirational leadership	✪✪✪✪
Maintenance leadership	✪✪✪
Change leadership	✪✪✪
Creative leadership	✪✪✪

6.27 | *Teaching responsibility*

Preparation Little.
Applicability All leaders.
Time taken A large amount.
Where/when Any and every opportunity that presents itself.

It is not enough to take responsibility. As a leader you also need to teach it. There is something faintly contradictory about saying that every problem is your problem and then teaching others to think in the same way. But it is a necessity. You cannot solve all of the problems of the world on your own. Well, I couldn't and I shall assume that you are human and fallible too. We need help.

Being seen to take responsibility for everything around you will have two opposite effects. On the one hand, you will act as a role model and encourage others to do the same. On the other hand, you will cause others to feel that they need not bother because it is now your responsibility.

There is a place for formal training in taking responsibility. How far you go down this path will depend upon the culture and resources of your organization.

Whether you train or not, you need to spread the word that taking responsibility is everyone's job. You need to find ways of increasing the role model aspects of your behaviour and decreasing the nannying side. The very best way to do this is to have a few discussions with people after you have sorted out a problem and ask them why they hadn't. Do not be tempted to do this before sorting it out because this defeats the point you are trying to convey.

So, each and every time you sort out a problem, find someone else who could have done it and discuss the situation with them. Make it clear that this issue was your responsibility, but it was also theirs.

Personal development   ✪
Inspirational leadership   ✪✪✪✪
Maintenance leadership   ✪✪✪
Change leadership   ✪✪✪
Creative leadership   ✪✪

6.28 | *Watch my feet, not my lips*

Preparation Buy a selection of Dilbert cartoon books (see Chapter 7).
Applicability All leaders.
Time taken A little time very, very often, a lot of time rarely.
Where/when Requires constant attention, so all of the time.

I have stressed and I will continue to stress that what you do is far more important than what you say. It doesn't matter how many pragmatic justifications you can generate for every action that you take in conflict with your stated beliefs, it is the actions that will endure, not the words. It takes only one slip to undo a huge amount of work so the first piece of advice here is, don't slip. You can't afford to.

As a leader you are human. You will make mistakes. In many instances you will be less aware of those mistakes than others around you. If you are able to, it is useful to have a confidante, someone who will let you know how your actions are seen by others. Ideally this should be a person with a great future behind them. In other words, someone who has a track record of success, so that you can trust them, but who has no ambition to move further, so that you can trust them.

Whether or not you can establish a confidante it is also necessary to get feedback directly from your people. The section 6.64 is about 360 degree feedback. This is something that is essential if you are to get a real picture of your actions. Making it truly anonymous and fairly widespread is also essential.

As an exercise, start by reading a selection of Scott Adams' Dilbert cartoons. Read them not from the Dilbert perspective (as most of us do), but accepting that you are the pointy-haired boss. Some, perhaps many, of your actions will be seen in this light. If you find these cartoons amusing it is probably because you have, or have had, a boss that you can identify in this role. Don't you find it scary that your people find these cartoons amusing?

Personal development	✪✪✪✪
Inspirational leadership	✪✪✪✪
Maintenance leadership	✪✪
Change leadership	✪✪✪
Creative leadership	✪✪✪

6.29 | *Conversations*

Preparation Read the next section (6.30) and prepare accordingly.
Applicability Any time you have specific or general messages.
Time taken A few minutes quite frequently.
Where/when Anywhere your people might be, any time.

The next section (6.30) is about communicating. Informal, face-to-face communication carries significantly more weight than any formal methods. Tactics for using the conversations you have are an essential part of your leadership armoury. Before you go rushing off to plan every 'chance' conversation for the next few days, it is also true that being seen to be selling a viewpoint is one of the fastest turn-offs in a conversation. Yes, another contradiction to overcome as a leader.

So, if I'm not talking about selling a particular viewpoint and I'm not talking about planning chance meetings, what am I talking about? In a word, preparedness. In order to use chance conversations to maximum advantage you must be prepared for them to happen. This means that you need a few, a very few, key messages that you want to drive home every opportunity you get.

A colleague once told me that he used the elevator test. If he could get his message across to someone he was sharing an elevator with, then it was short enough. What would your key elevator message be?

Having thought this through, develop a range of messages. People don't choose parrots for their leaders. You need to be seen to be thinking about this stuff.

Now you have the messages you must maximize the number of chance encounters. This is the tough part because the only way you can do this is to get up off your butt and walk out among your people. The more you are out of your office, the more face-to-face communication you are doing. The more of this you do, the more you are doing your job.

Personal development	✪
Inspirational leadership	✪✪✪
Maintenance leadership	✪✪✪
Change leadership	✪✪✪
Creative leadership	✪✪✪

6.30 | *Communicating*

Preparation An understanding of your vision, mission and goals.
Applicability Every leader.
Time taken At least a half day to start and then frequent short inputs.
Where/when Immediately and then inputs any time you can.

There is no point whatsoever in developing a set of strategies if the people who are to make them happen are not aware of them. There is no point whatsoever in having a vision for your business if the people who will put the fire into that vision don't know it. In short, all of the thinking you have done about driving your business forward needs to be communicated to the people who will provide the motive power.

A communication plan is the next logical step after working on strategy. You need to be thinking about your message as if it were a product. You could even think of it in traditional product terms: price, promotion, place and packaging.

Product – what is the product you are selling? Encapsulate this in a series of short and pithy statements that clarify the message for you. Try these out on others to ensure that you speak the same language. Get them to feed back to you what they've heard. Price – how can you get this message to people in a way that costs them the minimum in time and effort? Promotion – what will cause them to buy the message at all? Why will it interest them? Most importantly, what is in it for them? Place – what distribution methods do you have at your disposal? How could you increase these? Think creatively about new ways of conveying the message. Finally, packaging – why would they bother to pick up the message? What is the interest, the intrigue, the attraction that causes them to stop and pay attention?

I haven't seen communication plans described in these terms before, but for me a message is like any other product in a crowded market-place. It must be thought through from a wide range of dimensions.

Personal development	✪
Inspirational leadership	✪✪✪✪
Maintenance leadership	✪✪✪
Change leadership	✪✪✪
Creative leadership	✪✪

6.31 | *Knowing your competitors*

Preparation Learning to use the Internet.
Applicability All leaders.
Time taken A little, very often.
Where/when Any opportunity offered.

Information is power. Given the information sources that you have at your fingertips you should be an immensely powerful individual. The reason you are not comes in two parts. First, you haven't bothered to collect the information that you could. Second, you already know what isn't available. You need to bother and you need to accept that there is much more available than you would believe. A leader who isn't seen to have their finger on the pulse loses respect.

A first source of information should be the Internet (see Chapter 7). If you are in an industry with medium- to large-sized firms, then many of your competitors will have information on web pages. Trawl through these. If you don't use the Internet then you might want to consider finding out how to. Being too busy or too important may be an adequate reason, in your mind, for being a dinosaur, but there are many people who would disagree.

The press is always good. Getting hold of the press releases of your competitors is the very least you should be doing. Having press cuttings provided or searching the press yourself is also useful.

Then there is the information you can glean from the products of your competitors. What is their pricing strategy? Where are their products heading? How good is their design compared to yours? What other factors are they majoring on? What are the key similarities and key points of difference? Even in a commoditized market-place you can make these comparisons. My belief is that no product need be a commodity as long as you can think of creative ways to package, price or distribute it. Differentiation is always a key to success.

Finally, don't forget trade organizations and industry conferences. It always amazes me the amount that people are willing to tell you about their strategy as long as you are prepared to ask questions and are able to read between the lines.

Personal development	✪
Inspirational leadership	✪✪
Maintenance leadership	✪✪✪
Change leadership	✪✪
Creative leadership	✪✪

6.32 | **Knowing your customers**

Preparation None.
Applicability All leaders.
Time taken Little but often.
Where/when Any opportunity offered.

Customers are much like competitors in that they will tell you a great deal about themselves if you are prepared to ask in the right way.

There are two factors that will affect their willingness to help you. First, what's in it for them? In other words, how convinced are they that the information they give you will lead to a better service? Second, how easy do you make it for them? If there is a significant cost involved in giving the information they won't bother unless they really believe that there's a larger payback. Obviously, you can weight this relationship by bribing them – offering immediate payback for their help in a tangible way. Ultimately, the ideal should be to get the information flowing to you at no effort to your customers and without the need to bribe.

The example of SuperQuinn supermarkets in the Republic or Ireland springs to mind. They have customer suggestion boxes that are full to overflowing every day. They offer no bribes and there's no immediate benefit to doing this. What they do offer is a guarantee that every suggestion will be read the following morning by the meeting of the senior managers and that they will implement as many as they can as quickly as they can.

How can they afford to spend their time reading all of these suggestions? Well, if you had this free data flowing in about your customers' needs and wants you'd have to be a fool not to spend your time reading it. If you had the opportunity to duplicate this you'd have to be a fool not to take it up. Oh, you do have the opportunity and you haven't taken it up – sorry.

Finally, as well as asking them on paper, you should consider the other listening posts you can create. Your staff will know a lot about what works and what doesn't work for customers. Particularly those staff with daily, face-to-face contact. You yourself could learn more by spending time working on the face-to-face contact. Any opportunity, any time, take it.

Personal development	✪
Inspirational leadership	✪✪
Maintenance leadership	✪✪✪
Change leadership	✪✪✪
Creative leadership	✪✪

6.33 | **Knowing your people**

Preparation None.
Applicability All leaders.
Time taken Little, but very often.
Where/when Any opportunity offered.

If it is important that you know your customers, how much more important is it that you know the people who represent you to the customers? Your staff are the face of your organization. You must know the face that they are presenting. To know this you must know how they see and hear you (and your messages), and how they see the products and services you offer.

Some of the listening posts used for customers could be duplicated for staff. For instance, a suggestion box – with you guaranteeing to read the inputs on a daily basis and implementing as many as you are able – could be a huge source of information. The difficulty with this is that it is a promise you cannot afford to renege on.

A regular staff input survey is another source to consider. Asking a structured set of questions can give you an overview of the feelings of your staff, but it will not be a great source for a detailed picture. Asking the same questions time on time gives you a chance to compare how things are changing between surveys.

Talking to your staff is essential. In a large organization, prearranged sessions every so often might work, but there is nothing quite as effective as just getting out and about and talking to people. If you are doing this to spread your messages (see 6.29 *Conversations*) then you might want to stop and listen awhile as well as talking.

The real message is that any opportunity you can create to get input from your people direct, rather than filtered through managers or staff representatives, is an opportunity that you should seize with both hands.

Personal development	✪
Inspirational leadership	✪✪✪✪
Maintenance leadership	✪✪✪
Change leadership	✪✪
Creative leadership	✪✪

6.34 | *Knowing yourself*

Preparation None.
Applicability Everyone.
Time taken A lifetime (and more?).
Where/when Starting now and not stopping, ever.

Knowing yourself sounds easy but anyone who has started the journey to self-discovery will know that it is a very, very long road. Indeed it is probably never ending. I hold very strongly to the view that you cannot lead others until you can know yourself. Not completely, but better than most others know themselves.

This is a piece of self-development that really does benefit from outside help. It is possible on your own, but so much more difficult that you have to ask why you would want to make it that tough. Mind you, it is also true that even with some outside help, most self-discovery is a singular and personal process.

A good place to start is with a standard battery of psychometric tests. Understand from these what your behaviour preferences are and what impact these might have on others. Once you've done this, be prepared to treat the results lightly. These things are indicators. They are neither rigid science nor religion. If taken too seriously they can mislead and misdirect.

Another good place is to talk to family, friends and colleagues about what you do well and badly in interacting with others. If they are willing to be open with you, they could be a great source of insight. If they are not willing to be open with you, then you might glean some insight from this.

Looking inside yourself is a useful approach. Whether you do this through meditation, psychoanalysis or just some personal deep thinking is your business. You will need to think hard about your drivers and your motivation. Accept from the start that you are neither the hero you would like to be nor the demon you fear you might be, but that you are both an ordinary and an extraordinary person.

Personal development	✪✪✪✪
Inspirational leadership	✪✪✪
Maintenance leadership	✪✪
Change leadership	✪✪
Creative leadership	✪✪

6.35 | *How to be an ideal leader*

Preparation Read the rest of this book.
Applicability All leaders.
Time taken Ongoing.
Where/when Anywhere, any time.

In some ways this is what this whole book is leading towards. All of the previous and all of the subsequent sections are aimed at offering advice that will allow you to fulfil this aim. I wanted this section specifically because there are a couple of principles that don't fit easily elsewhere, but which sit over and above specific tips and techniques.

The overarching message is that leadership is about challenge and support. The very best leaders are those who make impossible demands and then offer impossible levels of support to help you to achieve.

The terms 'challenge' and 'support' need some explanation. They are subject to such a breadth of definition that they need to be fairly carefully handled.

Challenge This is not meant to imply that you challenge in an aggressive manner. It is not the notion of challenge normally associated with confrontation. It is meant more to imply that you have impossible targets to achieve. The managerial approach to this would be to break these targets down into a work plan and evaluate what could realistically be achieved in the time-scale. The leadership approach is to say that they are impossible but that the future of the business depends upon them so we either throw in the towel now or we commit to making them happen.

Support This is not meant to mean nannying or being overly gentle with people. It is meant to imply that in order to achieve impossible targets people need every obstacle that can be removed from their path removed. The managerial approach to this would be to offer a realistic set of resources in support of those meeting the targets. The leadership approach is to ask what you need to make this happen and then find ways of getting it there. It is about being there at all times for your people in a way that they know means that they can lean on you if they need to, but that they can't if they don't.

Personal development	✪
Inspirational leadership	✪✪✪✪
Maintenance leadership	✪✪✪
Change leadership	✪✪✪
Creative leadership	✪✪✪

6.36 | *How not to be a dunce*

Preparation None.
Applicability All leaders.
Time taken Ongoing.
Where/when Anywhere, any time.

In *Watch my feet, not my lips* (6.28) I mentioned Dilbert cartoons. Remember the pointy-haired boss? This is how many wannabe leaders are seen. Following some of the tips and techniques in this book will help you to avoid this, but there are a few simple steps that you should always have front of mind.

Do what you say you will do. Always. If you don't think you'll be able to achieve something, then say that you will try but might fail. Never promise something that you can't or might not be able to deliver. On those occasions where you promise and the world conspires against you to prevent it, be open about your failure.

Remember the fears that you have overcome. A few years ago, while designing a course in leadership, I went through a pilot version. It included the climbing wall and abseil that were obligatory a few years ago. I hate heights. The instructor demonstrated the absolute safety of the equipment. Afterwards he asked why I was scared. He had shown me it was safe. I explained that it wasn't a rational, logical thing. He explained that that is how it is for people who aren't used to taking the responsibility we, as leaders, thrust upon them. Logically they may know that they have safety equipment, but they are still scared. As experienced leaders we have overcome these fears and so fail to understand them in others.

Don't look for hidden motives. They might be there, but I have seen managers tying themselves in knots trying to interpret what was really meant by a particular action when it was nothing more than what it appeared on the surface.

Similarly, don't have hidden motives. Say what you are going to do and why you are going to do it. Many managers will hide their agendas for political reasons. The more open you are the more chance people have to follow you.

Personal development	✪
Inspirational leadership	✪✪✪✪
Maintenance leadership	✪✪✪
Change leadership	✪✪✪
Creative leadership	✪✪✪

6.37 | *Learning to learn*

Preparation None.
Applicability Everyone.
Time taken Half an hour.
Where/when Now.

It seems odd explaining how to learn. You've been doing it all of your life. Some of you will already have learnt how to learn and so this section will be irrelevant. A surprising number of people never learn how. For them, this might be useful.

The very best leaders are perpetual students. They never stop learning.

Not everybody learns in the same way. It is true that for most people the old adage, 'I hear and I forget; I see and I remember; I do and I understand', holds true. But how you hear, see and do is a very personal process.

I am a person who likes to get straight in and play with a new idea, but who can't really use it well until I've understood the idea and everything that sits behind it. This means that I must do a huge amount of research about everything I get involved with, just to fill in the background. For many others, this is irrelevant.

Look at *Becoming a figure of eight person* (6.63) and fit yourself to a preferred type. In general, the Dynamic Masculine approach will be not to bother with learning. Where it is unavoidable they will want it to be useful and usable very quickly. The Dynamic Feminine approach will be to grab hold of an idea and play with it – often stretching it to and beyond its limits. When excited by a new concept they will spend time on it, otherwise they'll move on swiftly. The Static Feminine approach will be to take time and trouble over absorbing ideas and will prefer to learn in the company of others. The Static Masculine approach will be to study hard and absorb as much detail as possible. They will be the ones who actually read computer manuals.

Think hard about your learning style. Figuring out the best way for you to absorb information will be key to future success.

Personal development	✪✪✪✪
Inspirational leadership	✪✪
Maintenance leadership	✪✪
Change leadership	✪✪
Creative leadership	✪✪

6.38 | *Reward*

Preparation None.
Applicability All leaders.
Time taken Ongoing.
Where/when Infrequent consideration of where you stand.

In my mind there is a difference between reward and recognition. This section covers reward, the next recognition. Reward, for me, has an element of money involved in it. Recognition is often cheaper and more effective.

The first and most obvious reward that you offer is the pay packet. How much do you pay your people in relation to the average for your sector? I am a firm believer in the adage, 'Pay peanuts, get monkeys'. In general, if you show that you value people by paying a reasonable wage, then they appreciate it. Naturally, this is not enough on its own and you'll need to do a whole range of other things in this book to reap real rewards. This need not mean that you are at the top of the tree for pay. Make sure that you are being fair and then motivate using something other than money.

The next element of reward are those payments that happen, contractually, for extra time or unsociable hours; overtime payments, shift payments and the like. In recent years there has been a trend in some industries to reduce or remove these payments and yet still push people to work overtime. Naturally, this causes resentment and that is not a good basis from which to lead. Again, fairness would be the watchword here.

Finally, reward could include money that you pay for anything else that your staff do. Payment for good ideas for instance. This is where I have a personal prejudice that recognition is a far, far better tool. I have no research to back me up on this, but it just feels more right to me.

Personal development	✪
Inspirational leadership	✪✪✪
Maintenance leadership	✪✪✪
Change leadership	✪✪
Creative leadership	✪✪

6.39 | **Recognition**

Preparation Buying of gifts or creating stationery.
Applicability All leaders.
Time taken Ongoing.
Where/when Everywhere.

Birthdays Set up a database of the birthdays of all staff in your area and make sure that they receive a birthday card from their manager just before their birthday.

BravoGrams Print a 'cheque-book' for each manager which contains BravoGrams or Brownie Points or whatever name you think fits. Have them liberally sprinkle these about the place whenever they catch someone doing something almost right. Write thank-you letters to your own people.

Giveaways Have each of your managers stock a drawer, or small cupboard, with gifts such as calculators, pens, T-shirts, memo pads, etc. Encourage them to give these away whenever they feel that someone has put extra effort into their work. Make specific 'Awards for the Month' where the gift is relevant to the reason for the award.

Hall of Fame Set up a Hall of Fame – pictures and names of staff who have done something special for your customers and keep it up to date – there is nothing sadder than a Hall of Fame where half the staff have left.

Get-togethers Hold formal and informal social gatherings. These may be as trivial as a coffee-and-doughnut session or as formal as a meal at the Ritz (or maybe not …).

Listen! Being listened to is often the most real form of recognition that leaders can offer their staff. Make opportunities for unstructured listening and for complaints and suggestions. Make notes, promise action, feed back what has been said, deliver. Be prepared to ask dumb questions – the boss does not have to know everything. Be involved in what you're listening to – you are more likely to remember what's said if you listen wholeheartedly.

Talk! Talk to your people. Tell them you appreciate what they've done for you and for the business. Be specific. Let them know why it matters to you.

The 'trick' The easy trick to remember with recognition is that there isn't one. It takes continuing effort. Once started it becomes habit forming and improves results.

Personal development   ✪
Inspirational leadership   ✪✪✪✪
Maintenance leadership   ✪✪✪
Change leadership   ✪✪✪
Creative leadership   ✪✪

6.40 | *Saying 'No'*

Preparation None.
Applicability All leaders, particularly those who find 'no' a tough word.
Time taken Half an hour to a lifetime.
Where/when In any conversation or negotiation.

Most people who become leaders have little trouble in saying no to others. This lack of assertion often does not apply. Some, however, find themselves in a leadership role and then find that their job is impossible because they have agreed to things they should never have said yes to.

If there is even the remotest chance that this describes you then read on.

There are many reasons why people find saying no difficult. They mostly stem from being brought up to be polite and accommodating. Learning to be assertive, and realizing that you have the right not to do as others want you to, is a huge step towards making this easier. There is something about the socialization process of girls in many families that makes it even tougher for women managers and leaders to be assertive.

Here are some quick tips.

Accept that you have the right to say no and that anyone who pushes or manipulates you to try to change your mind is infringing your rights.

Accept that others have the right to ask you for help, but that you can choose to give it or not according to your needs, not theirs.

If you anticipate a particularly tough negotiation, visualize it going your way. Role play the conversation that you want to have and make sure that things go as you want.

Learn to be persistent in asking for what you want and saying what you are prepared to offer. Repeating yourself (even over and over and over again) can be a useful technique.

Be prepared to offer or accept compromises that give you what you want, even when (or especially when) they give the other party more, too.

Stay calm. You are sticking to your rights, what need do you have to get angry?

If you have a severe problem in this area take some assertiveness training. It will pay huge dividends. If you have a minor problem, then train yourself by reading books about assertiveness.

Personal development	✪✪✪
Inspirational leadership	✪✪✪
Maintenance leadership	✪✪✪
Change leadership	✪✪
Creative leadership	✪✪

6.41 | *Personal development*

Preparation None.
Applicability All leaders.
Time taken A lifetime.
Where/when Starting now, everywhere, any time.

There are many elements of developing you as a person that this book can't hope to cover. The more fully developed you are as a person, the more you will act as an inspiration to those you lead. Each way that you find to develop yourself, over and above those in this book, will add another element to your already impressive character.

One thing that you should do early on is to understand what you are good at and what you are not good at. You will want to develop both because, although getting rid of weaknesses is important, getting better at what you are good at is pretty important, too. (See 6.66 *Your personal strengths and weaknesses*.)

Do not think about personal development in terms of the job you do or even in terms of the jobs you want to do in the future. Your development is not a job-related thing it is a life-related thing (see 6.65 *Life, don't talk to me about life*). Your job, even this role as a leader that you are developing yourself for, is a small part of you. There is so much more and your development should reflect that. Rather like the ancient Samurai in Japan, you should view your social development and your artistic development as intrinsic to your technical development. Find ways to become a whole person.

One way to start that is to ask yourself whether you have a long-cherished ambition that you will never fulfil. Have you always wanted to paint? Have you always wanted to learn to play the piano? Whatever it might be, why not do it? Sign up for classes and just learn how to do what you want to do. You really are never too old. The interesting thing is that you will be better at your job if you round out your personality.

Personal development   ✪✪✪✪
Inspirational leadership   ✪✪
Maintenance leadership   ✪✪
Change leadership   ✪✪
Creative leadership   ✪✪

6.42 | *Selecting the right people*

Preparation Further courses or reading.
Applicability All leaders.
Time taken A few days at least – probably much longer.
Where/when Starting some time before you need a new team member.

A leader is only as good as their team. Great leaders have a great team around them, others surround themselves with people who are no threat. If they are no threat they are no help either.

For those in an established role this is a long-term strategy. You will already have a team. Developing them is a priority (see 6.50 *Developing others*). As and when you have an opportunity to recruit into the team, look for someone who is good enough to step into your job. That's the calibre of person you need.

So, how do you know how good they are? The first thing you must do is to learn how to interview well. The face-to-face interview is the most compelling element of the battery of techniques you have available to you in selection. Some informal research I did a few years ago on graduate recruitment showed that, of a two-day intensive selection process, the face-to-face interview was the only significant indicator of whether they would be taken on or not. This isn't to say that it was necessarily the best, just that against it, none of the other elements mattered. There are some excellent texts on interviewing and some good courses, too. For me, one of my most important lessons was to trust my intuition. On those occasions when my gut said don't take them, my head said do and I listened to my head, I always ended up regretting it. Always.

Before you ever get to interview, though, you must know what sort of person you are looking for. What skills do they need (really need)? What sort of personality must they have to fit in the team? What can you offer them other than the job? Think this through well and you'll be half way to getting the right person.

Personal development	✪
Inspirational leadership	✪✪✪
Maintenance leadership	✪✪✪✪
Change leadership	✪✪✪
Creative leadership	✪✪

6.43 | *Energy*

Preparation None.
Applicability All leaders.
Time taken Ongoing.
Where/when Any time, any place.

Leaders are like that bunny in the battery commercials. Not cute, pink and fluffy (necessarily), but they just keep on going and going and going and going.

This level of endurance and commitment is part of the inspiration that you will be offering. How can you create this additional energy to make sure that you are there whenever you are needed?

The first thing to do is to make sure that you are physically and mentally fit. For physical fitness, see 6.44 *Get fit*. For mental fitness, work on the self-development throughout the book, but mostly make sure that you are doing what you love. If the work that being a leader in this role entails does not give you a real buzz, then you're in the wrong job. If you don't leap out of bed in the morning ready to face the challenges, then you're in the wrong job. Mind you, if you don't dash home every evening, eager to get on with your life, then you're also in the wrong job (or possibly the right job but the wrong life).

In an attempt to evaluate what would make this job perfect for you, try thinking of the absolute ideal job for you. It might be real and it might be fictional. List all of the attributes of this job. When I say all, I mean all – cover at least an A4 sheet and ideally more. Now, for each of those attributes, list the equivalents in your own. What needs to change? There's probably something. So, how do you change it? It may mean changing jobs. It probably means changing the shape of the job that you do.

Another tip is to ensure that you are only using your energy on what's necessary. See 6.23 *Mastering time* and 6.62 *Being ubiquitous*.

Finally, I have mentioned Tai Chi a couple of times in this book. There are some disciplines like this that manage energy in a much subtler way than coarse physical exercise. They would be well worth trying to see how they work for you.

Personal development	✪✪✪✪
Inspirational leadership	✪✪✪
Maintenance leadership	✪✪✪
Change leadership	✪✪✪
Creative leadership	✪✪✪

6.44 | *Get fit*

Preparation None.
Applicability Anyone.
Time taken A few hours a week.
Where/when At prearranged sessions.

First let me stress that I am not talking about becoming an Olympic athlete. Fitness is about being fit for purpose. That is no different for you than for a product you might sell. In this instance it means being fit enough to do your job. The more sedentary your job, the more you'll need to work on your fitness in order to do it.

The first thing to establish to become fit is an attitude of mind. Push yourself to do a few things that stretch you physically a little. Walk to a few places that you might have taken the car. Take stairs instead of lifts. At the weekend, work a little harder at something physical like gardening, or even walking the dog. As with all advice about fitness, if you suspect that any of this will put your body under stress – ie, if you are overweight or have a physical problem – consult your doctor for advice.

Next, think about (and then *do* something about) a regular programme of physical activity. Join a gym or take up the sport that you dropped when you were younger – cricket, football, hockey, netball. If it's darts then think again, this probably doesn't qualify. Swimming is an ideal form of exercise in that it is relatively gentle and uses a large amount of your body. Many pools offer early morning sessions for people on their way to work.

Schedule the activity in a way that you will continue it. On the way to work, on the way home from work or at lunchtime are timings that work well. Make sure that you have at least two sessions a week. Any exercise that is lighter but repeated more frequently, is better than heavier and less often.

Personal development	✪✪✪✪
Inspirational leadership	✪
Maintenance leadership	✪
Change leadership	✪
Creative leadership	✪

6.45 | *Culture*

Preparation Select a representative group of your people.
Applicability All leaders.
Time taken Half a day to establish – years to change.
Where/when Pretty damned soon.

Culture means a wide range of things. It is one of those words that can subtly adapt its meaning depending upon how you use it. In this context I mean the culture of your organization and, by that, I mean 'how we do things around here'.

The culture of an organization is one of the subtlest, least measurable and yet most important aspects of what makes it work or makes it fail. Finding out what the culture is and changing it are tough.

There are no easy tests to establish the current culture, but a technique that I like is to look at rules. I run a session with a cross-section of the people in an area and start by asking for ideas that would get you fired. These often start with the obvious, 'Switching off vital equipment', etc, but soon move on to the less obvious, 'Being caught in bed with the boss's partner', etc. The more of these that you uncover, the more feel you will have for what's going on.

The next question to ask the representative group is, 'What are the rules around here'. Again you will start with the obvious set of rules that come straight from the rule-book but, with prompting, you'll move on to how we have to dress, the hours we're expected to work, the ways we're expected to behave.

Finally you could ask explicitly, 'How do we do things around here?'. This is a tougher one to answer and so people may dry up unless you prompt them, so think in advance of some examples of your own.

The outputs from these questions will give you the shape and feel of the culture of your organization. The next stage is to think about what you would like it to be. Describe for yourself your ideal picture of your organization working. Contrast that with the picture you got from the earlier questions. Look for major anomalies first and think about what would need to change to move to your ideal. You're in charge – change it.

Personal development	✪
Inspirational leadership	✪✪✪✪
Maintenance leadership	✪
Change leadership	✪✪✪✪
Creative leadership	✪✪✪

6.46 | *Creating change*

Preparation Reading on creativity and change.
Applicability All leaders.
Time taken Ongoing.
Where/when Starting soon and never ending.

Much of what we've been talking about has involved change happening in your organization. To be sure, much has also involved changes in you, but those are your problem: we'll look at the organizational change here.

Change is an odd thing. There are sayings around like, 'The only person who welcomes change is a wet baby', and yet anyone who lives without it feels as though they are stagnating. On the other hand, there is a general feeling of fear around change. It often feels as though we have lost something, but it takes time to realize what we have gained.

The shape of the business world means that change is inevitable. It always has been, but the periods between changes are becoming shorter and shorter until it seems a continuous process. As leader you have two jobs in this process. First, designing the shape of the changes and second, making them happen.

To design the shape of the changes you will need to become creative. Don't worry that is far easier than you might imagine. Just read *Instant Creativity* (Paul Birch and Brian Clegg). The techniques available to help with creative idea generation and problem solving are easily learnt and implemented.

Making change happen is tougher. The reason for the change will be obvious to you. It will be far more obvious to others why they should not. Convincing people to change has two elements. Showing them the negatives of where they are and showing them the positives of where they could be. Okay, so there's more than just showing them. They will cling like limpets to what they know and will avoid what they don't. You have to be pretty damned convincing.

Once you have started the process of change, monitor it and ensure that it moves continually forward. Given half a chance, inertia will creep in and the change will halt.

Finally, given the nature of change I described earlier, you'll need to be starting the next one before this one is even under way.

Personal development	✪
Inspirational leadership	✪✪✪✪
Maintenance leadership	✪
Change leadership	✪✪✪✪
Creative leadership	✪✪✪✪

6.47 | *Leading a team over time*

Preparation None.
Applicability All leaders.
Time taken Ongoing.
Where/when Ongoing.

There are many texts on teamworking or leadership that make you feel that it's like climbing a mountain. You have a peak to ascend but once you have reached the top, that's it, your task is done. Unfortunately leadership isn't like that. It's more akin to climbing an infinite mountain with no summit. The climb goes on for ever and you never reach the top. You cannot ever sit back and say, 'My work here is done'.

Okay, that's not entirely true because there will come a time when you want the challenge of a steeper slope and you choose to hand this one on to someone else. That doesn't mean that you've reached the top, just that the gradient isn't challenging enough.

The main tool that you have for providing motivation and enthusiasm is the vision. That isn't to say that you wave this in front of people and tell them to be enthused. Rather, this drives your energy and enthusiasm and that transfers into the business. If you find this waning, stop and ask yourself why. Is the vision no longer inspiring? Is the business no longer a challenge? What more do you want in your life and what do you need to do to get it?

Assuming that you are still inspired by the vision (see 6.12), then your leadership task is to move towards it. Having a really tough mission (see 6.13) to try for is one step. If you get close to this then change it. Having the ideal mix in your team (see 6.42) is another. As your needs change, so should the team. The communication (see 6.29 and 6.30) that keeps them focused is key.

Having done that, much of your role is to get out of the way and let them achieve. Keep up the challenge, keep up the support. Continually monitor the temperature. Continually monitor success. But mostly, step back.

Personal development   ✪
Inspirational leadership   ✪✪✪✪
Maintenance leadership   ✪✪✪✪
Change leadership   ✪✪✪
Creative leadership   ✪✪✪

6.48 | *Honesty is the best policy*

Preparation None.
Applicability All leaders.
Time taken Ongoing.
Where/when Ongoing.

Honesty is the best policy – a great aphorism and one that we choose to ignore much of the time. Business ethics is becoming big business. Teaching people how to be ethical, or in some cases teaching people how to appear to be ethical, is a growth industry. How can this be? How can you need to be taught basic values? I think that the answer is that fudging issues, half truths and avoidance have become so common-place that we accept them as normal business practice. Just a few weeks ago I found myself defending someone's actions in what I regard to be morally indefensible cir-cumstances and using the phrase, 'But that sort of behaviour has become normal business practice'. I stopped myself and took a step back, admitted what I really felt and apologized for the slip, but even so I surprised myself. I have always had a very strong personal moral code. It often gets in my way, but I stick by it. Yet in business, it seems, I am more willing to compromise. It's almost as though because it's business these aren't real people.

It seems to be similar in politics. People will indulge in activities that they would find unacceptable in their private lives, but seem to use the notion of the end justifying the means or some notion of a greater good. In my view this is just so much bull. The means are part of the end. If what you do requires you to act in a way that you regard as wrong, then what you do is wrong. If you still want to do it that's your choice, but don't pretend to yourself that the ethical basis is sound.

My advice on this, for what it is worth, is always to tell the truth. Communicate to your people and your customers more than you are comfortable communicating. Any half truth that you hide behind will come back to bite you later. You will become known as untrustworthy and that is no basis at all for good leadership.

Personal development	✪
Inspirational leadership	✪✪✪
Maintenance leadership	✪✪✪
Change leadership	✪✪
Creative leadership	✪✪

6.49 | *Decisions, decisions, decisions*

Preparation None.
Applicability All leaders.
Time taken A small amount over a week and then ongoing.
Where/when Soon and then ongoing.

Many years ago, when I first became a manager, I took a Diploma in Management Studies. One of the exercises I clearly remember involved all those on the course measuring the time they spent on various activities. The discussion, once we'd done the measurement, centred around the notion that a manager's role was about making decisions. When we looked at our results we were extremely embarrassed. None of us had taken any time making decisions during the week that we had measured. Indeed, I had spent a measurable (not significant, but still measurable) amount of time fixing a printer. My role could more honestly be described as printer repairer rather than decision maker.

We argued about this and said that the actual process of making decisions was embedded in the role and took no time. So we were then asked to list all of the decisions we'd made during that week. This became even more embarrassing because they all fell into the trivial and not worth mentioning area. Hardly the stuff of major business titans. Years later, at a very senior level within an organization, with hundreds of staff spread around the world, I still found that my role wasn't about minute-to-minute, day-to-day decisions. It was about driving forward major decisions that I'd already made and then keeping out of the way.

In order to understand your decision-making profile try monitoring yourself for a week and keep a note of every decision you make. I would suggest that at the end of this process you remove the trivial and then note how much of your time is genuinely spent making decisions. My contention is that this is not at the heart of the leadership role, whatever belief we may have cherished for years. Decisions are necessary to make things happen and you will be relied upon to make the decisions sometimes. The more you can force the decision back to those working for you, the more you will develop them and fulfil your true leadership role.

Personal development	✪✪
Inspirational leadership	✪✪✪
Maintenance leadership	✪✪✪
Change leadership	✪✪
Creative leadership	✪✪

6.50 | *Developing others*

Preparation None.
Applicability All leaders.
Time taken A few weeks elapsed, less actual.
Where/when Starting soon and then ongoing.

You do what you do as a leader only through others. Yes, you are the one that gives them direction. You are the one that motivates and drives them. But they produce your products, they serve your customers. They do it.

If you don't work on developing your people, then you are not enhancing the potential of your greatest resource.

The first thing you must do is to establish the development needs of your people. This is traditionally done by a human resources department establishing job role capabilities and then measuring people against these capabilities. My view is that this is, and always has been, a total waste of effort. It gives comfort because it feels rigorous, but in practice it ends up being precisely wrong rather than roughly right.

A good place to start with development is with the people who are to be developed. What do they feel they need? If you were to offer them money to train themselves in anything they wanted to do, what would it be? If it turned out to be flower arranging, rather than the design of administration systems, is that wrong? It might be, but only you can decide. If you have managed to fire people up with the need and the drive to work towards your vision, then my view is that they will ask for appropriate development. For sure there will be a few who try to take you for a ride and will want to develop themselves in preparation for leaving you to work elsewhere, but this may actually be a cost-effective way of moving them out while still having them feel positive about you.

Finally, don't think of developing people only in terms of training. The business books you give them, the things you ask people to do and the example that you set will also significantly add to their development.

Personal development	✪
Inspirational leadership	✪✪✪✪
Maintenance leadership	✪✪✪
Change leadership	✪✪✪✪
Creative leadership	✪✪✪✪

6.51 | **Networking**

Preparation None.
Applicability All leaders.
Time taken Ongoing.
Where/when Ongoing.

A few years ago I heard Tom Peters speaking about managing yourself and he was saying that there are two fundamental tools – your resumé and your Rolodex. In other words, what you have achieved and who you know. This is more true for a leader than for anyone else. You need a strong network to support and help the work that you are doing.

The way that your network changes over time is a key measure of its success. Who are you adding and where are they from? If your key contacts are from within your organization, then you are being too insular. If they are from within your industry, then you are being too insular. You need to find ways to expand your network beyond its current limitations.

Every day you should be adding a new contact (OK, let's average that to five a week) and at least two-thirds of those should be from outside your organization, with a fair proportion from outside your industry.

How can you make this happen? I guess the obvious first answer is get out more. Spend time at conferences. If they are conferences that are nothing to do with your industry then so much the better. Use these conferences as opportunities to chat to people and to swap business cards. If your card is memorable this will help you to stick in their mind. I used to have the job title Corporate Jester (for British Airways) – that was memorable. Now my cards are printed on playing cards because I don't do business, I play. The 'Pick a card, any card' line is also memorable.

After you have met people, follow up on those you like. Invite them to dinner or arrange to meet them for no better reason than to get to know them better. It is not only fun, it is great for your network and your personal development.

If you are the sort of person who finds this sort of socializing difficult then push yourself. Push at the point when you meet people in the first place and push again to make the follow-up happen. It becomes habit forming and consequently easier over time.

Personal development	✪✪✪✪
Inspirational leadership	✪✪
Maintenance leadership	✪✪
Change leadership	✪✪
Creative leadership	✪✪

6.52 | *Measurement*

Preparation None.
Applicability All leaders.
Time taken Initially a couple of days and then ongoing.
Where/when Soon and then ongoing.

What gets measured gets done. So, measure what you want done and all of your problems are solved.

No, I didn't think you'd buy that straight away. There are a few issues to resolve first. First, what do you measure? For most businesses the answer to this is to measure what is easy to measure. This goes back to the notion of being precisely wrong rather than roughly right. This has resulted in many businesses measuring input not output.

In general, inputs are easy to measure. When do you turn up? When do you leave? What overtime do you do? Outputs are tougher. What do you add to the business? What do you produce? What is the value of what you produce? What hole would you leave if you went tomorrow?

An ideal measurement system would be one that started with your vision (see 6.12), your mission (see 6.13) and your goals (see 6.14) and derived measures as movement towards them. These measures are not just financial. Indeed, if the financial measures are more than a quarter of those you end up with, I would suggest it is because you are sticking to what is easy. So, take some time to design an ideal measurement system for your vision, mission and goals. Don't worry about what is and what is not measurable, imagine that you can know everything. Include up to 50 measures at this stage.

If you now had to cut these measures down to about a dozen which would you choose? It may be that you need to invent new ones that are indicators or aggregates of a number of the others. Now, of these dozen measures which are currently available? Which are possible and which are impossible? Now, what can you do to take a guess at or an estimate of the impossible ones? It is rare that you can't get an indicator.

OK, now make it so.

Personal development	❂
Inspirational leadership	❂❂
Maintenance leadership	❂❂❂
Change leadership	❂❂❂
Creative leadership	❂❂

6.53 | *Destroying the system from the inside*

Preparation None.
Applicability All leaders (particularly those within large organizations).
Time taken Ongoing.
Where/when Ongoing.

You are responsible for the bureaucracy and the inefficiencies in the area you lead. It's no use bleating on about the demands of the parent company or the needs of the wider organization. If there is something going on that doesn't add directly to the achievement of your vision, then it is getting in the way and it is your fault.

The title of this section is deliberately provocative. I have long held the view that part of the role of a leader is to encourage an underground movement that will question the leadership and be a real thorn in the side. It sounds perverse to suggest that you should have a hand in creating problems for yourself, but this is one of the few ways that you will generate real questions. Real questions, from people who share your vision but not necessarily your ways of going about them, are the ones most worth hearing. So, one way of destroying the system is allowing or encouraging the creation of a dissenting voice.

Another way is to hold a high-profile event aimed at identifying and removing wasted activities. If you added up the minutes taken to generate the product or service you offer and then the minutes available from your total workforce, you will find a huge discrepancy. Often twice or three times the time available to time needed. Sometimes far more. All of this difference happens because of systemic inefficiencies. Some of these are unavoidable (or would cost more to remove than they are worth) but many of them can and should be expunged.

Having done this you need some way of every employee being able to question wasted time. Ultimately, the ideal would be a culture that said if you don't think it adds to the vision don't do it. This would put the onus on you to explain those things that do add, but not obviously.

Personal development	✪
Inspirational leadership	✪✪✪
Maintenance leadership	✪
Change leadership	✪✪✪✪
Creative leadership	✪✪✪✪

6.54 | *Creating a team*

Preparation None.
Applicability All leaders of teams.
Time taken Initially a few days with some ongoing effort.
Where/when Now and ongoing.

Whether you have a team of three or of three thousand there is work to be done in making that group into an effective team. We have talked about choosing the people in your team (see 6.42 *Selecting the right people*) but the bonding process, the process of creating connections between them, takes more than just a set of jobs.

Traditional team-building exercises focus on stretching individuals until something bends or breaks, or on having a good time together. I have never believed in pushing people to or beyond their limits. I do believe in having fun, but this is only part of the answer. What, for me, is key is a sense of connectedness between team members. Since most team-building takes place away from the office, there is then also a need to take it back into the workplace.

I would see effective team-building in four stages:

1. Breaking down barriers through energetic, fun, warmup exercises (*Instant Teamwork* by Paul Birch and Brian Clegg – see Chapter 7)
2. Making connections by slowing things down and allowing more person-to-person, eye-to-eye, heart-to-heart contact
3. Sharing or gift giving, where individuals or groups show the value of others
4. Planning the transfer back into the workplace.

In general, I would see this as a team-building event of some sort that leads to an atmosphere of working for and in support of the team as a whole. The feeling generated by the team-building event would need to be developed through any activities planned in stage four, above, and anything else that you decide to do in support of the development of your team.

Personal development	✪
Inspirational leadership	✪✪✪
Maintenance leadership	✪✪✪✪
Change leadership	✪✪✪
Creative leadership	✪✪

6.55 | *Keeping abreast*

Preparation None.
Applicability All leaders.
Time taken A few minutes to an hour a day.
Where/when As suits your routine.

A key to business success in the 21st century is an ability to handle knowledge (for more read Brian Clegg's *Instant Brainpower* – see Chapter 7). Knowing more and being able to access that information faster than your competitors. There are those who argue that this skill is being made redundant by computers – they will be able to sift and sort information so fast that you will not need to know anything except how to switch them on. While this may be true in the future (a pretty distant future, it seems to me) my view is that information overload will get worse before it gets better.

How can you know more? How can you absorb more than you already do?

The first thing to do is to set aside more of your time for learning. Yes, it seems that I am asking you to create huge amounts of time out of nothing but remember 6.19 *Delegation* – if your people are doing all of your work, you'll have plenty of time.

The next thing to do is to get better at using that time. You can do this in four ways. First, read faster – train in speed reading or simply push yourself to get through more in less time. Second, remember more – learn better ways of note-taking or practise recalling items that you have read in order to improve retention. Third, read more digested material – if someone is going to go to the trouble of digesting business or news items then it seems impolite not to read them. Finally, expand your view of learning to include listening to educational radio shows, browsing on the Internet or attending lectures.

Personal development	✪✪✪✪
Inspirational leadership	✪✪
Maintenance leadership	✪✪
Change leadership	✪✪
Creative leadership	✪✪

6.56 | **Memory**

Preparation None.
Applicability All leaders.
Time taken A few minutes practice every now and then.
Where/when Any opportunity.

You must have seen those naff newspaper advertisements, 'Have you ever wished you had a better memory?'. They work on the fact that most people have wished just that. The sad thing is that everybody could have a better memory just by following a couple of tricks that are really very simple. Sad, because not many people seem to bother even when they know them.

Starting with names. You forget names because you don't bother to remember them. That isn't just a twist of the words. Often you will have forgotten the name within minutes of being told it. This is because you have not transferred it from the short-term memory in your head to the long-term. If you have remembered it for more than a few minutes and then forgotten it, this is because you have not built paths to the memory that will allow you to recall it. In order to cope with both of these ways of forgetting, repeat the name when you are introduced. Then, after the introduction, say the name to yourself a few times while associating it with the face. Make a point of using the name. Later, recall the name and the face as a way of reinforcing the path to the memory.

What about phone numbers? You forget these because the human brain was never built to remember them. It evolved to cope with a 3D, multi-sensory world, not the abstract world of numbers. Use one of the many rhyming methods to transfer numbers from the abstract to the real and then build a vivid story around the resulting words.

For more information on these, and other ways to improve your memory, see Brian Clegg's *Instant Brainpower* (see Chapter 7).

Personal development	✪✪✪✪
Inspirational leadership	✪✪✪
Maintenance leadership	✪✪
Change leadership	✪✪
Creative leadership	✪✪

6.57 | *Bureaucracy – and how to develop it*

Preparation Collect a week's in-tray and example customer communications.
Applicability All leaders.
Time taken An hour or two.
Where/when As soon as you have the paperwork.

Bureaucracy is a dirty word in most businesses. Usually with good reason. But bureaucracy can be a real plus for your business if it is handled right and if it is treated with a high degree of caution.

In order to complete this exercise and the next, you will need to save a week's-worth of the mail that travels through your in-tray. This could be the originals or copies. You will also need to collect together as many samples as you can of the bureaucracy that you send to your customers.

Having collected this material, go through it item by item and identify any input that is required from you in association with this item. What is the information that you are being asked for? What action are you being asked to take? When you are asked for this, are there more efficient ways (for you) of providing it than the one being requested?

Now look through the information you are asking for, from your customers. Ask yourself the same questions? How could you make their lives easier?

As a case in point, you might want to look at the various bookstores on the Internet. They don't use paper, but still need the bureaucracy. They all need to ask you for a certain amount of information, but some will ask this every time you make an order. Others will store this information and allow you to insert it automatically using a password. The most advanced, and the one that I use most often, assumes that you are the only person to use your PC and allows you to buy with a single click. The item is charged to your usual card and sent to your usual address. It makes buying from them worryingly easy!

Personal development   ✪
Inspirational leadership   ✪✪
Maintenance leadership   ✪✪✪
Change leadership   ✪✪✪
Creative leadership   ✪✪

6.58 | *Bureaucracy – and how to kill it*

Preparation Exercise 6.57.
Applicability All leaders.
Time taken An hour or two.
Where/when As soon as you have completed the previous exercise.

There are times when bureaucracy exists only for the benefit of the bureaucrats who generate it. This sort should be killed as soon as possible. Any leader worthy of the title will spend time rooting out the career bureaucrats from within their organization in order to minimize future paper generation.

Even before you root them out you should get rid of their paperwork. After conducting the previous exercise, ask yourself what would be the effect on you of doing nothing with this form or that paper? What would you lose as a result?

If you can see no benefit to it then send it back to the originator with a request to justify your return of the information. What is in it for you?

If you can see benefit to providing a subset of the information, then provide it, ask the person who generates it what is the benefit to you of providing the rest. Obviously, for internally generated bureaucracy, the question needs to ask for the benefit to you and to the business as a whole.

For those pieces of bureaucracy that are information providers rather than requesters, ask yourself what benefit you gain from the information. All of it, item by item. If none, then send it back and explain that you don't want it any more. If it is internally generated, then send it back with a request to justify why it is produced and what it adds to the bottom line. I have run a few departments that were responsible for providing information within a large organization. One thing I tried was to stop the production of all regular reports and then only to reinstate them for those who complained. It was surprising, even to the cynic in me, how many of them were never missed by any of their recipients.

Personal development	✪
Inspirational leadership	✪✪
Maintenance leadership	✪✪✪
Change leadership	✪✪✪
Creative leadership	✪✪

6.59 | *Being unreasonable*

Preparation None.
Applicability All leaders.
Time taken 10 minutes.
Where/when Now or any time you can spare.

Much of my take on leadership throughout this book has been about love. This may have led some to believe that I want everybody to love you if you are to be a leader. This may cause you to think that you need to be nice to people.

There is no necessary relationship between being liked and being a good leader. Being respected may be an essential, but this doesn't come from being nice.

A good leader makes unreasonable requests of people (including themselves) and then offers unreasonable levels of support to allow these requests to be met. This means that at times a leader will be disliked, perhaps even hated, by their people. If you are the sort of person who wants to be liked by others (and many of us are), then you will need to consider what effect this dislike will have upon you. Are you prepared to take it? If not, then you might not be ready to be a leader.

Management is about being reasonable. It is perfectly possible to be a manager and to be liked by your people. This, for many, is the deciding factor in whether they lead or manage. Leadership requires an inner resilience that will allow you to take the flak that results from being unreasonable and allows you to continue to say, 'Yes, I know that it is unreasonable and yet I still require it of you. What do you need to make it happen?'.

To uncover your own feelings about this, try this short exercise. List for yourself 10 of the key achievements you have made in the last year that have involved other people as a resource. Rate on a scale of 1 to 10 how possible this achievement seemed when you started. (1 = totally possible, 10 = absolutely impossible). It is likely that the closer your score is to 100 the less reasonable you are in your requests. Provided that the support you have given your people is outstanding then this is not a bad position for a leader to be in.

Personal development   ✪
Inspirational leadership   ✪✪✪✪
Maintenance leadership   ✪✪
Change leadership   ✪✪✪✪
Creative leadership   ✪✪✪

6.60 | *Being a hero*

Preparation Exercise 6.2 *Being an inspiration.*
Applicability Any leader who is led by principles and passion.
Time taken Initially an hour.
Where/when When you are ready.

Being a hero is similar to, yet different from, being an inspiration (see exercise 6.2 *Being an inspiration*). Many of the aspects of being inspirational are required before you can move to heroism, but this requires something more. This requires that you lead from the front in a way that demonstrates that your principles and passions are more important than your career or personal ambitions. Think hard about your driving forces before you travel this road because this is not something that you can bluff. If your beliefs are not this fundamental then pass this exercise by.

Start by identifying what it is about your organization that gets in the way of your principles and passions becoming reality. What actions would it take on your part to remove these obstacles?

Next, identify whether or not taking these actions would damage others around you. Have you prepared them for this possibility? If not, then in what ways can you protect them from the fallout of your actions?

Now there is nothing left to do but to make your principles and passions a reality. This will involve both conflict and risk. That is the nature of being led by something more than just the bottom line. The potential for payoff from this is high in terms of creating the role and environment you desire. The potential for damage is high in terms of losing your job or limiting your career potential.

Personal development	✪
Inspirational leadership	✪✪✪✪
Maintenance leadership	✪✪
Change leadership	✪✪✪
Creative leadership	✪✪✪

6.61 | ***Being obsessive***

Preparation Exercises 6.12 and 6.16.
Applicability All leaders.
Time taken Half an hour.
Where/when Anytime.

In the previous exercise I majored on the notion of being driven by your personal principles and passions in the business. This is where true leadership arises. This is also the source of the obsession featured in this exercise.

Before you can do this you need to be very clear what it is that drives you. If it is the bottom line of the business, then your obsessions will vary according to the current mood and flavour of the business gurus. If it is something deeper than this, then you may well find business and leadership success despite the ups and downs of the latest fads.

To identify the source of your passion you need to decide what it is that gets you out of bed and into work in the mornings. For some it is the wage. For others it is something much deeper. If you have trouble with this then exercises 6.12 *Vision* and 6.16 *Values* may be of assistance. You may want to try the collage exercise in 6.12, but with a particular focus on your personal vision rather than the business.

Having identified your passions and your principles it is worth taking some time to decide how much they contribute or detract from the success of your business. If they detract from the business, what could you alter in order to change this? It is possible, for instance, that one of your personal beliefs is to give back to society in the form of charity or direct help? This will detract from the bottom line but, with the correct tax treatment and some use of PR, could actually contribute. It is perfectly OK to have principles and passions that do not contribute as long as you are truly in charge of the business. If not, then you need to consider the owners (shareholders?) whose wealth you are using.

The final element of being obsessive is to make every judgement from a position of principle and for everything you do to be driven by your passion.

Personal development   ✪✪
Inspirational leadership   ✪✪✪✪
Maintenance leadership   ✪✪
Change leadership   ✪✪✪
Creative leadership   ✪✪

6.62 | *Being ubiquitous*

Preparation None.
Applicability All leaders.
Time taken A little time, very often.
Where/when Everywhere and all of the time.

The very best leaders can be a pain in the neck for their people because they are forever popping up all over the place. They are well informed – in fact they are absurdly well informed. They seem to be driving every major initiative. Mostly they are clearly at the heart of the drive of the business. In short, they get everywhere all of the time.

This is obviously impossible. So, how can you give this impression?

You need to plan very carefully where you go and what you do when you are there. It is relatively easy to be ubiquitous in a small company. In a large one you must make sure that you spread yourself evenly and thinly.

Take out your schedule for the next two months and look at how your time is spent relative to the geography of your people. If you are spending a significant proportion of your time in one place this should be because the significant majority of your people are there. If this is not true, then work to balance where and when you carry out business in order to even it up.

The next thing to ensure is that you are seen. When you travel to other locations it is useless to lock yourself away in an office. Walk the shop floor and meet people. Shorten the formal meetings and hold more informal ones.

Finally, you need to ensure that you are absurdly well informed about the goings-on in the company. Think through how you could establish a series of listening posts that will get you this information. Once you have them, think through how you will bring your information into informal conversations. It is important not only to be everywhere and know everything, but to be seen to be everywhere and to know everything.

Personal development	✪
Inspirational leadership	✪✪✪
Maintenance leadership	✪✪✪
Change leadership	✪✪✪
Creative leadership	✪✪✪

6.63 | *Becoming a figure of eight person*

Preparation None.
Applicability Any time.
Time taken A few minutes.
Where/when Wherever.

In his book, *Masculine and Feminine* (now out of print), Gareth Hill develops some of Jung's thoughts on personality into a figure of eight diagram that sets the dimensions of Dynamic – Static (Doing – Being) and Masculine – Feminine alongside one another.

Masculine

| Static
Masculine | Dynamic
Masculine |

Static   **Dynamic**

| Static
Feminine | Dynamic
Feminine |

Feminine

The masculine and feminine are personality traits and are not related to your gender.

	POSITIVE	IMAGE	NEGATIVE	IMAGE
Static Masculine	Ordered, protective, responsible	King Arthur, Queen Elizabeth I	Dictatorial, controlling, killjoy	Traffic warden or petty official
Dynamic Feminine	Creative, transformative, positively destructive, tolerates ambiquity	Kali, Merlin, an artist	Madness, negatively destructive, chaos for chaos sake	Caligula, The Furies, The witches in Macbeth
Static Feminine	Nurturing, compassionate, generous, selfless	Mother Teresa, Father Christmas	Smother love, suffocating addictive	Lady Macbeth, Gollum in Lord of the Rings
Dynamic Masculine	Courageous, heroic, expansive, ambitious	Jason, Alexander, Emily Pankhurst	Aggressive, ruthless, tyrannical	Lucrecia Borgia, Attila the Hun

Movement through the quadrants follows the figure of eight. Most people have a preferred style. A well-rounded individual will be able to operate in all areas. Many people stick to a particular style and find it hard to move. Seeing the negative aspects of the current quadrant encourages you to move on. Seeing the negative of the next quadrant encourages you to stay put. The circle in the centre is seen as a particular area of risk. It is tougher to cross from top left to bottom right, or bottom left to top right, than from top right to top left, or bottom right to bottom left. This may well be because both dimensions change at this crossover.

Look at the descriptive words above and ask yourself where you sit most comfortably. Where is your area of least comfort? Do you move freely? If not, which areas do you need to practise in order to be more willing to move into them?

One of the areas of least comfort for many people is the Dynamic Feminine. Some of the exercises in *Instant Creativity* (see Chapter 7) will help to develop comfort in this area.

Personal development	✪✪✪✪
Inspirational leadership	✪✪
Maintenance leadership	✪✪
Change leadership	✪✪
Creative leadership	✪✪

6.64 | *360-degree appraisals*

Preparation Finding a suitable 360-degree feedback mechanism.
Applicability All leaders who haven't already done this.
Time taken Varies from minutes to a day or more.
Where/when Anytime you feel ready.

I was keen to include an exercise on 360-degree appraisals because they are an important way of understanding how you are seen, compared to how you see yourself. There is no sensible way of making this exercise complete within this book. You need to find an appraisal tool that you can use to help you to understand yourself, your strengths and your weaknesses as a leader.

The 360-degree appraisal is simply asking anyone you work for, some people that you work with, some people that work for you, and yourself, what you are good at and what you are not so good at. The methodologies used for doing this vary widely.

There are many instruments on the market that will assist in this. If you work for a large organization then they probably already have one. At the lowest end it will consist of other people listing what you do well and what you do badly. At the highest end it will be packed with pseudo-science and norms and all sorts of spurious statistics. There are a few fundamentals that I feel are important.

First, any 360-degree feedback should be anonymous. This is a big advantage in having it conducted by an outside agency that can be convincingly detached compared with your secretary or your HR/Personnel manager. Second, the feedback should be primarily directed at leadership. There are many ways of measuring that are directed at middle management. Much of what you would discover from this would be useless. Third, it should cover a range of attributes. Finally, an ideal feedback exercise would be able to take you to the next stage of deciding whether or not you wished to change as a result of the feedback and, if you did, how you would go about doing so.

Personal development ✪✪✪✪
Inspirational leadership ✪✪
Maintenance leadership ✪✪
Change leadership ✪✪
Creative leadership ✪✪

6.65 | *Life, don't talk to me about life*

Preparation None.
Applicability Everyone.
Time taken 30 minutes initially and then many months or years.
Where/when Starting now.

As you will have gathered if you have worked through this book to arrive at this point, leadership is not about what you do so much as who and how you are. Getting a life is a key to this.

Take some time now to examine your life. We all have different reasons for working. For some it is purely instrumental; merely a way of providing the funding for a life outside of work. At the other extreme are those for whom work is their life; nothing outside it is of any significance to them. Neither of these groups will ever make great leaders. There is a need for a combination of a passion for the business and a passion for life (and this means life outside of the business).

Write out an agenda for a typical week. If you don't have such a thing, then spot the trends in your time. Do you have a family? When do you spend time with them? Do you have hobbies? When do you spend time doing them? When do social events tend to happen? When do you arrive at the office, when do you leave? How much time do you spend travelling? Once there, what sorts of things happen during the week that you enjoy or that you hate?

Once you have mapped out an imaginary but representative week, take a look at it. What items in this schedule would you like to spend more time doing? What items would you like to drop or minimize? What doesn't appear on here that you have always dreamt should be there? Listen most to this last item. All of us have long-sublimated dreams that we have learnt to ignore because we are living in the real world. Part of getting a life is accepting that you are able to shape the real world to meet your needs and wants. So, listen to your dreams.

OK, now for the easy bit. Completely redesign your life so that it reflects the ideal rather than the current schedule. Well, it may not be easy but it is certainly possible. You don't believe so today, but take a small item that you want to change and work on that first. Having succeeded at this, move up to bigger and bigger items. Then stop and examine your life once more.

Personal development	✪✪✪✪
Inspirational leadership	✪
Maintenance leadership	✪
Change leadership	✪
Creative leadership	✪

6.66 | *Your personal strengths and weaknesses*

Preparation Exercise 6.64 *360-degree appraisals*.
Applicability Anyone who has read this book.
Time taken 20 minutes.
Where/when As soon as possible after reading the book.

Many of the exercises in the book have been about identifying and addressing your personal strengths and weaknesses. These have been from a specific angle. This one is aimed at finishing with an overview of further work needed.

As you go through this you will be tempted merely to read it through and answer the questions in your head. Don't do this. Write down answers and think hard about the questions being asked. This stuff is important to you.

Start by listing those things that you think are genuine strengths. What do you do well? Do you have any evidence for this? What impact does this strength have on your ability to lead?

Next, list those things that you need to improve upon. What lies behind this weakness? What evidence do you have for this? What impact does this have on your ability to lead? Remember, only you see what you write down so be as honest as you can.

If you have already conducted the 360-degree appraisal exercise, go over the results of that now. If you have any other input on your style from other sources, look at those now. What strengths and weaknesses would you add from the input of others? What effect would these have on your ability to lead?

Your task now is to remove those weaknesses that you choose to do something about and to build on those strengths that you feel could be enhanced further. The one trap that you might fall into is regarding the strengths as being more important than the weaknesses and so spending too much time on them.

Look at the contents of this book. Are there exercises that you have skimmed that might help in this development? If not, look at Chapter 7 for further resources that might help you. Beyond this you need to grasp every opportunity that presents itself to develop out of your weaknesses and increase the range of your strengths.

Personal development   ✪✪✪✪
Inspirational leadership   ✪
Maintenance leadership   ✪
Change leadership   ✪
Creative leadership   ✪

7

OTHER SOURCES

THERE'S MORE

Instant Leadership is merely a taster to get you started on the leadership road or to give you a boost along it if already started. To develop further you will need to live your life as a leader. This short chapter is a resource kit for going beyond *Instant Leadership*. In parts it is aimed at the leadership role and in parts at developing you as a person.

THEORY

In putting together the *Instant* series of books our focus has been on the practical. We have tried to steer clear of the theory underlying the exercises. If you would like to explore more of the theory, check the Creativity Unleashed on-line bookshop at **http:/ /www.cul.co.uk/books**, which provides plenty of information and direct buying links to the biggest on-line bookshops in the US and the UK. It's also worth checking there for more up-to-date references, and for books that are hard to get hold of in the UK.

BOOKS

LEADERSHIP BOOKS

Warren Bennis and Burt Nanus *Leaders*, Harper Business, 1986
They describe a range of different leaders (many in unexpected roles like an orchestra conductor) and say what makes leadership work, or not.

Peter Block *The Empowered Manager*, Jossey-Bass, 1987
A really great book. I personally rate Peter Block and rate this book.

Peter Drucker *The Effective Executive*, Butterworth-Heinemann, 1988
Another classic, the one that you have to have read if you've read anything on leadership.

John Harvey-Jones *Making It Happen*, HarperCollins, 1994
Troubleshooter on paper. Simple, straightforward advice.

Joseph Jaworski and Betty Flowers *Synchronicity: The Inner Path of Leadership*, Berrett Koehler, 1998
A book that is more about life than about leadership and is therefore probably one you should read.

John Kotter *The Leadership Factor*, The Free Press, 1998
One of the classics in the area. Well worth reading.

James McGregor Burns *Leadership*, Harper & Row, 1978
A book about transformational leaders – those who look to develop new ways of seeing the world rather than just manage what is.

OTHER BOOKS FOR SUBJECTS MENTIONED IN THE TEXT

Scott Adams *The Dilbert Principle*, HarperCollins, 1996
Scott Adams *Dogbert's Top Secret Management Handbook*, HarperCollins, 1996
These and any of the other Dilbert books available will give you a tangential view of how leadership is not, should not and must not be (but all too often is) done.

Paul Birch and Brian Clegg *Instant Creativity*, Kogan Page, 1999
Add creative sparkle to the leadership mix.

Paul Birch and Brian Clegg *Instant Teamwork*, Kogan Page, 1998
A quick guide to time-outs, warm-ups and ice-breakers to change the shape and feel of your meetings and get-togethers.

John Cassidy, B C Rimbeaux and Diane Waller *Juggling for the Complete Klutz*, Klutz Press, 1995
The best-ever book to learn to juggle from. It starts with simple exercises like dropping things and moves up to keeping things in the air. Has the bonus of a free set of bean bags.

Brian Clegg *Instant Brainpower*, Kogan Page, 1999

Brian Clegg *Instant Time Management*, Kogan Page, 1999

Brian Clegg *Mining the Internet*, Kogan Page, 1999

The three best books written on these subjects. Am I biased because he's a friend? Well, yes I am. I still stick by this assessment.

Robert Kaplan and David Norton *The Balanced Scorecard*, Harvard Business School Press, 1996
The pair who developed the concept of the balanced scorecard – an alternative to the traditional financially driven business measurement systems.

ON-LINE LEADERSHIP

As always, the Internet can be a useful source of information. The one caveat is that any links that are suggested in a book will quickly become out of date. Using a search engine such as **http://www.digital.altavista.com** or **http://yahoo.com** will allow you to find links of your own, but you will need to make your search specific in order not to be overwhelmed by responses.

Some references that might stay current are listed below.

http://www.leader-values.com
This is a really useful site that aims 'to become one of the best meeting places for leadership and value systems on the net'.

http://www.pfdf.org
The Drucker Foundation. A wide-ranging site with a large selection of articles and other information.

http://www.LTWorks.com
Leadership That Works. This is mostly an advertisement so is of little value, but the charisma test at **http://www.LTWorks.com/charisma** might be of interest.

http://www.ee.ed.ac.uk/~gerard/MENG/ME96/Documents/Intro/leader.html
A page looking at the difference between management and leadership.

http://www.ohr.psu.edu/jed/lindholm.htm
A Penn State University site on leadership.

http://www-cgsc.army.mil/cal/index.htm
The Center for Army Leadership. For a view of how leadership is seen in the US military. It also has some book reviews on more general leadership.

APPENDIX:
THE SELECTOR

This appendix contains a set of tables that will help you to find the activity that best suits your needs. The first entry is a random selector. This can be effective if you aren't sure where to start, or you feel you are getting stuck in a rut. The next set of tables are sorted by the star ratings for each activity, to make it easy to pick out (say) a personal development activity. Finally, there are tables sorted by preparation time and time taken.

THE RANDOM SELECTOR

Take a watch with a second hand and note the number the second hand is pointing at now. Take that number activity from the list of 60 below. The activities in the list exclude a few that are very demanding in terms of time. This gives you a way of dipping into activities and doesn't work you through the book sequentially.

No.	Ref.	Title	No.	Ref.	Title
1	6.1	Charisma	30	6.31	Knowing your competitors
2	6.2	Being an inspiration	31	6.32	Knowing your customers
3	6.3	Getting your inspiration	32	6.33	Knowing your people
4	6.4	Technical competence	33	6.34	Knowing yourself
5	6.5	Learning to love your business	34	6.36	How not to be a dunce
			35	6.37	Learning to learn
6	6.6	Learning to love your customers	36	6.38	Reward
			37	6.39	Recognition
7	6.7	Learning to love your staff	38	6.40	Saying 'No'
8	6.8	Learning to love your suppliers	39	6.42	Selecting the right people
			40	6.43	Energy
9	6.9	Learning to love yourself	41	6.44	Get fit
10	6.10	Leadership and management	42	6.45	Culture
			43	6.46	Creating change
11	6.12	Vision	44	6.47	Leading a team over time
12	6.13	Mission	45	6.48	Honesty is the best policy
13	6.14	Setting goals	46	6.49	Decisions, decisions, decisions
14	6.15	Developing a business plan			
15	6.16	Values	47	6.50	Developing others
16	6.17	Using stress	48	6.51	Networking
17	6.18	Diaries	49	6.52	Measurement
18	6.19	Delegation	50	6.54	Creating a team
19	6.20	Meetings – and how to chair them	51	6.55	Keeping abreast
			52	6.56	Memory
20	6.21	Meetings – and how to develop them	53	6.57	Bureaucracy – and how to develop it
21	6.22	Meetings – and how to kill them	54	6.58	Bureaucracy – and how to kill it
22	6.23	Mastering time	55	6.59	Being unreasonable
23	6.24	Learning to relax	56	6.60	Being a hero
24	6.25	Sleep well	57	6.61	Being obsessive
25	6.26	Taking responsibility	58	6.62	Being ubiquitous
26	6.27	Teaching responsibility	59	6.63	Becoming a figure of eight person
27	6.28	Watch my feet, not my lips			
28	6.29	Conversations	60	6.64	360-degree appraisals
29	6.30	Communicating			

ACTIVITIES IN PERSONAL DEVELOPMENT ORDER

This table sorts the activities by the personal development star rating. Those at the top have the highest star rating, those at the bottom the lowest.

Ref.	Title	Ref.	Title
✪✪✪✪		6.49	Decisions, decisions, decisions
6.1	Charisma	6.61	Being obsessive
6.2	Being an inspiration		
6.3	Getting your inspiration	**✪**	
6.5	Learning to love your business	6.11	Strategy
6.6	Learning to love your customers	6.14	Setting goals
6.7	Learning to love your staff	6.15	Developing a business plan
6.8	Learning to love your suppliers	6.16	Values
6.9	Learning to love yourself	6.20	Meetings – and how to chair them
6.17	Using stress	6.21	Meetings – and how to develop them
6.18	Diaries		
6.24	Learning to relax	6.22	Meetings – and how to kill them
6.25	Sleep well	6.27	Teaching responsibility
6.28	Watch my feet, not my lips	6.29	Conversations
6.34	Knowing yourself	6.30	Communicating
6.37	Learning to learn	6.31	Knowing your competitors
6.41	Personal development	6.32	Knowing your customers
6.43	Energy	6.33	Knowing your people
6.44	Get fit	6.35	How to be an ideal leader
6.51	Networking	6.36	How not to be a dunce
6.55	Keeping abreast	6.38	Reward
6.56	Memory	6.39	Recognition
6.63	Becoming a figure of eight person	6.42	Selecting the right people
6.64	360-degree appraisals	6.45	Culture
6.65	Life, don't talk to me about life	6.46	Creating change
6.66	Your personal strengths and weaknesses	6.47	Leading a team over time
		6.48	Honesty is the best policy
		6.50	Developing others
✪✪✪		6.52	Measurement
6.4	Technical competence	6.53	Destroying the system from the inside
6.19	Delegation		
6.23	Mastering time	6.54	Creating a team
6.40	Saying 'No'	6.57	Bureaucracy – and how to develop it
✪✪		6.58	Bureaucracy – and how to kill it
6.10	Leadership and management	6.59	Being unreasonable
6.12	Vision	6.60	Being a hero
6.13	Mission	6.62	Being ubiquitous
6.26	Taking responsibility		

ACTIVITIES IN INSPIRATIONAL LEADERSHIP ORDER

This table sorts the activities by the inspirational leadership star rating. Those at the top have the highest star rating, those at the bottom the lowest.

Ref.	Title
✪✪✪✪	
6.2	Being an inspiration
6.3	Getting your inspiration
6.12	Vision
6.13	Mission
6.26	Taking responsibility
6.27	Teaching responsibility
6.28	Watch my feet, not my lips
6.30	Communicating
6.33	Knowing your people
6.35	How to be an ideal leader
6.36	How not to be a dunce
6.39	Recognition
6.45	Culture
6.46	Creating change
6.47	Leading a team over time
6.50	Developing others
6.59	Being unreasonable
6.60	Being a hero
6.61	Being obsessive
✪✪✪	
6.1	Charisma
6.5	Learning to love your business
6.6	Learning to love your customers
6.7	Learning to love your staff
6.8	Learning to love your suppliers
6.9	Learning to love yourself
6.10	Leadership and management
6.11	Strategy
6.16	Values
6.19	Delegation
6.20	Meetings – and how to chair them
6.21	Meetings – and how to develop them
6.22	Meetings – and how to kill them
6.29	Conversations
6.34	Knowing yourself
6.38	Reward

Ref.	Title
6.40	Saying 'No'
6.42	Selecting the right people
6.43	Energy
6.48	Honesty is the best policy
6.49	Decisions, decisions, decisions
6.53	Destroying the system from the inside
6.54	Creating a team
6.56	Memory
6.62	Being ubiquitous
✪✪	
6.4	Technical competence
6.14	Setting goals
6.15	Developing a business plan
6.18	Diaries
6.23	Mastering time
6.31	Knowing your competitors
6.32	Knowing your customers
6.37	Learning to learn
6.41	Personal development
6.51	Networking
6.52	Measurement
6.55	Keeping abreast
6.57	Bureaucracy – and how to develop it
6.58	Bureaucracy – and how to kill it
6.63	Becoming a figure of eight person
6.64	360-degree appraisals
✪	
6.17	Using stress
6.24	Learning to relax
6.25	Sleep well
6.44	Get fit
6.65	Life, don't talk to me about life
6.66	Your personal strengths and weaknesses

ACTIVITIES IN MAINTENANCE LEADERSHIP ORDER

This table sorts the activities by the maintenance leadership star rating. Those at the top have the highest star rating, those at the bottom the lowest.

Ref.	Title
✪✪✪✪	
6.14	Setting goals
6.15	Developing a business plan
6.20	Meetings – and how to chair them
6.21	Meetings – and how to develop them
6.22	Meetings – and how to kill them
6.42	Selecting the right people
6.47	Leading a team over time
6.54	Creating a team
✪✪✪	
6.4	Technical competence
6.10	Leadership and management
6.11	Strategy
6.12	Vision
6.13	Mission
6.18	Diaries
6.19	Delegation
6.23	Mastering time
6.26	Taking responsibility
6.27	Teaching responsibility
6.29	Conversations
6.30	Communicating
6.31	Knowing your competitors
6.32	Knowing your customers
6.33	Knowing your people
6.35	How to be an ideal leader
6.36	How not to be a dunce
6.38	Reward
6.39	Recognition
6.40	Saying 'No'
6.43	Energy
6.48	Honesty is the best policy
6.49	Decisions, decisions, decisions
6.50	Developing others
6.52	Measurement
6.57	Bureaucracy – and how to develop it

Ref.	Title
6.58	Bureaucracy – and how to kill it
6.62	Being ubiquitous
✪✪	
6.1	Charisma
6.5	Learning to love your business
6.6	Learning to love your customers
6.7	Learning to love your staff
6.8	Learning to love your suppliers
6.9	Learning to love yourself
6.16	Values
6.28	Watch my feet, not my lips
6.34	Knowing yourself
6.37	Learning to learn
6.41	Personal development
6.51	Networking
6.55	Keeping abreast
6.56	Memory
6.59	Being unreasonable
6.60	Being a hero
6.61	Being obsessive
6.63	Becoming a figure of eight person
6.64	360-degree appraisals
✪	
6.2	Being an inspiration
6.3	Getting your inspiration
6.17	Using stress
6.24	Learning to relax
6.25	Sleep well
6.44	Get fit
6.45	Culture
6.46	Creating change
6.53	Destroying the system from the inside
6.65	Life, don't talk to me about life
6.66	Your personal strengths and weaknesses

ACTIVITIES IN CHANGE LEADERSHIP ORDER

This table sorts the activities by the change leadership star rating. Those at the top have the highest star rating, those at the bottom the lowest.

Ref.	Title	Ref.	Title
✪✪✪✪		**✪✪**	
6.45	Culture	6.1	Charisma
6.46	Creating change	6.5	Learning to love your business
6.50	Developing others	6.6	Learning to love your customers
6.53	Destroying the system from the inside	6.7	Learning to love your staff
6.59	Being unreasonable	6.8	Learning to love your suppliers
		6.9	Learning to love yourself
		6.16	Values
✪✪✪		6.31	Knowing your competitors
6.2	Being an inspiration	6.33	Knowing your people
6.3	Getting your inspiration	6.34	Knowing yourself
6.10	Leadership and management	6.37	Learning to learn
6.11	Strategy	6.38	Reward
6.12	Vision	6.40	Saying 'No'
6.13	Mission	6.41	Personal development
6.14	Setting goals	6.48	Honesty is the best policy
6.15	Developing a business plan	6.49	Decisions, decisions, decisions
6.19	Delegation	6.51	Networking
6.26	Taking responsibility	6.55	Keeping abreast
6.27	Teaching responsibility	6.56	Memory
6.28	Watch my feet, not my lips	6.63	Becoming a figure of eight person
6.29	Conversations	6.64	360-degree appraisals
6.30	Communicating		
6.32	Knowing your customers	**✪**	
6.35	How to be an ideal leader	6.4	Technical competence
6.36	How not to be a dunce	6.17	Using stress
6.39	Recognition	6.18	Diaries
6.42	Selecting the right people	6.20	Meetings – and how to chair them
6.43	Energy	6.21	Meetings – and how to develop them
6.47	Leading a team over time	6.22	Meetings – and how to kill them
6.52	Measurement	6.23	Mastering time
6.54	Creating a team	6.24	Learning to relax
6.57	Bureaucracy – and how to develop it	6.25	Sleep well
6.58	Bureaucracy – and how to kill it	6.44	Get fit
6.60	Being a hero	6.65	Life, don't talk to me about life
6.61	Being obsessive	6.66	Your personal strengths and weaknesses
6.62	Being ubiquitous		

ACTIVITIES IN CREATIVE LEADERSHIP ORDER

This table sorts the activities by the creative leadership star rating. Those at the top have the highest star rating, those at the bottom the lowest.

Ref.	Title
✪✪✪✪	
6.46	Creating change
6.50	Developing others
6.53	Destroying the system from the inside
✪✪✪	
6.3	Getting your inspiration
6.14	Setting goals
6.19	Delegation
6.26	Taking responsibility
6.28	Watch my feet, not my lips
6.29	Conversations
6.35	How to be an ideal leader
6.36	How not to be a dunce
6.43	Energy
6.45	Culture
6.47	Leading a team over time
6.59	Being unreasonable
6.60	Being a hero
6.62	Being ubiquitous
✪✪	
6.1	Charisma
6.2	Being an inspiration
6.5	Learning to love your business
6.6	Learning to love your customers
6.7	Learning to love your staff
6.8	Learning to love your suppliers
6.9	Learning to love yourself
6.10	Leadership and management
6.12	Vision
6.13	Mission
6.15	Developing a business plan
6.27	Teaching responsibility
6.30	Communicating
6.31	Knowing your competitors
6.32	Knowing your customers
6.33	Knowing your people

Ref.	Title
6.34	Knowing yourself
6.37	Learning to learn
6.38	Reward
6.39	Recognition
6.40	Saying 'No'
6.41	Personal development
6.42	Selecting the right people
6.48	Honesty is the best policy
6.49	Decisions, decisions, decisions
6.51	Networking
6.52	Measurement
6.54	Creating a team
6.55	Keeping abreast
6.56	Memory
6.57	Bureaucracy – and how to develop it
6.58	Bureaucracy – and how to kill it
6.61	Being obsessive
6.63	Becoming a figure of eight person
6.64	360-degree appraisals
✪	
6.4	Technical competence
6.11	Strategy
6.16	Values
6.17	Using stress
6.18	Diaries
6.20	Meetings – and how to chair them
6.21	Meetings – and how to develop them
6.22	Meetings – and how to kill them
6.23	Mastering time
6.24	Learning to relax
6.25	Sleep well
6.44	Get fit
6.65	Life, don't talk to me about life
6.66	Your personal strengths and weaknesses

ACTIVITIES IN ORDER OF EASE OF PREPARATION

This table sorts the activities by the ease with which you can prepare for them. Those at the top need no preparation and those at the bottom need significantly more.

Ref.	Title	Ref.	Title
6.2	Being an inspiration	6.65	Life, don't talk to me about life
6.5	Learning to love your business	6.4	Technical competence
6.6	Learning to love your customers	6.19	Delegation
6.7	Learning to love your staff	6.22	Meetings – and how to kill them
6.8	Learning to love your suppliers	6.24	Learning to relax
6.10	Leadership and management	6.27	Teaching responsibility
6.16	Values	6.1	Charisma
6.17	Using stress	6.3	Getting your inspiration
6.18	Diaries	6.9	Learning to love yourself
6.25	Sleep well	6.12	Vision
6.26	Taking responsibility	6.13	Mission
6.32	Knowing your customers	6.14	Setting goals
6.33	Knowing your people	6.15	Developing a business plan
6.34	Knowing yourself	6.20	Meetings – and how to chair them
6.36	How not to be a dunce	6.21	Meetings – and how to develop them
6.37	Learning to learn	6.23	Mastering time
6.38	Reward	6.28	Watch my feet, not my lips
6.40	Saying 'No'	6.29	Conversations
6.41	Personal development	6.30	Communicating
6.43	Energy	6.31	Knowing your competitors
6.44	Get fit	6.39	Recognition
6.47	Leading a team over time	6.45	Culture
6.48	Honesty is the best policy	6.46	Creating change
6.49	Decisions, decisions, decisions	6.60	Being a hero
6.50	Developing others	6.61	Being obsessive
6.51	Networking	6.35	How to be an ideal leader
6.52	Measurement	6.42	Selecting the right people
6.53	Destroying the system from the inside	6.57	Bureaucracy – and how to develop it
6.54	Creating a team	6.58	Bureaucracy – and how to kill it
6.55	Keeping abreast	6.64	360-degree appraisals
6.56	Memory	6.66	Your personal strengths and weaknesses
6.59	Being unreasonable	6.11	Strategy
6.62	Being ubiquitous		
6.63	Becoming a figure of eight person		

ACTIVITIES IN ORDER OF TIME TAKEN

This table sorts the activities by the time that they take. Those at the top save you time and those at the bottom take significantly more.

Ref.	Title	Ref.	Title
6.20	Meetings – and how to chair them	6.1	Charisma
6.21	Meetings – and how to develop them	6.2	Being an inspiration
		6.11	Strategy
6.22	Meetings – and how to kill them	6.12	Vision
6.5	Learning to love your business	6.13	Mission
6.6	Learning to love your customers	6.14	Setting goals
6.7	Learning to love your staff	6.15	Developing a business plan
6.8	Learning to love your suppliers	6.27	Teaching responsibility
6.16	Values	6.30	Communicating
6.17	Using stress	6.35	How to be an ideal leader
6.23	Mastering time	6.36	How not to be a dunce
6.25	Sleep well	6.38	Reward
6.59	Being unreasonable	6.39	Recognition
6.63	Becoming a figure of eight person	6.42	Selecting the right people
6.66	Your personal strengths and weaknesses	6.43	Energy
		6.44	Get fit
6.10	Leadership and management	6.45	Culture
6.18	Diaries	6.46	Creating change
6.19	Delegation	6.47	Leading a team over time
6.24	Learning to relax	6.48	Honesty is the best policy
6.28	Watch my feet, not my lips	6.49	Decisions, decisions, decisions
6.29	Conversations	6.50	Developing others
6.31	Knowing your competitors	6.51	Networking
6.32	Knowing your customers	6.52	Measurement
6.33	Knowing your people	6.53	Destroying the system from the inside
6.37	Learning to learn		
6.40	Saying 'No'	6.55	Keeping abreast
6.54	Creating a team	6.62	Being ubiquitous
6.56	Memory	6.65	Life, don't talk to me about life
6.57	Bureaucracy – and how to develop it	6.3	Getting your inspiration
		6.4	Technical competence
6.58	Bureaucracy – and how to kill it	6.9	Learning to love yourself
6.60	Being a hero	6.26	Taking responsibility
6.61	Being obsessive	6.34	Knowing yourself
6.64	360-degree appraisals	6.41	Personal development